# FINDING PROFITABLE DEALS

## The Real Estate Investor Manuals
## Volume II

GABRIELLE DAHMS

Data provided here is deemed to be accurate but NOT guaranteed. The contents imply neither legal nor financial advice. Readers are encouraged to consult appropriate professionals and do their homework. The author is not responsible now or in the future for any liability, loss, or risk incurred as a result of the use of any of the information contained in this book.

All opinions and remaining spelling or grammatical mistakes are those of the author.

This is a non-fiction work.

For FREE reports and blog posts, visit www.Riches-in-Niches.com.

# DEDICATION

*For all those who aim to be the best they can be.*

# Table of Contents

# PREFACE

Profitable real estate deals are the lifeblood of successful real estate investing. That much is obvious. But what is a deal? And where do you find one?

I wrote this book as a sequel to my book *How Trends Make You A Smarter Investor*, a book about conscious and conscientious real estate investing.

While the first book delved into nine big trends, every real estate investor ought to know, it did not address how best to find profitable real estate. *Finding Profitable Deals* picks up the slack.

The book contains various real estate investment vehicles. It helps to identify great markets and real estate bargains. Beyond that, it features a marketing overview and a resource section.

Other books and courses about real estate investments exist. Many investment niches warrant their own books. As a real estate professional of almost two decades, I wrote this book as an overview. My clients inspired me to do so.

I want to stimulate your desire for more and to inspire you to excel in the real estate investment that best aligns with you. The book's content reminds novice and veteran investors that real estate investments opportunities affect people and societies.

May your real estate investing make a positive difference in all areas of your life–and in those of others!

# INTRODUCTION

Over the years real estate investors continue to ask questions like "where to find the best real estate bargains," "what markets are the best markets." Variations on that theme proliferate in real estate investing and in real estate.

The need to understand the markets and to analyze them arises alongside questions about where to locate such deals. This is true because many investors only look at investment price tags, at least in the beginning.

Investment price tags represent one metric, though a somewhat deceptive one. For example, many properties in, say, the mid-West, appear to be fantastic deals to investors who live in much higher property value states. Yet, often such properties do not represent value for a variety of reasons.

Questions about the best real estate markets to invest in and how to identify and find profitable real estate investments stymie many investors.

Some never get off the ground in real estate investments, which remain a dream versus reality. Others search around, sometimes find something that works for them, but often after a steep learning curve. Such a learning curve costs time, money, energy, and effort.

And then there are those who succeed right away or almost right away. What distinguishes those investors?

This book proposes that what distinguishes successful real estate investors from those who are not and from those who remain dreamers is their ability to recognize, find, and acquire profitable real estate investments. To do so these investors need to know:

- What qualifies as a profitable real estate investment?
- Which real estate investment categories are available?
- What specific real estate investment categories require?
- Where real estate investment opportunities exist?
- How to analyze real estate investment offerings?
- How to acquire profitable real estate investments?
- How to set up real estate investing as a business?

Discussions about real estate investing fundamentals such as financing, investor mindset, and due diligence are important.

*Finding Profitable Deals* focuses on locating real estate investments While information about these subjects shows up here, this book repeats essential information on these topics but not all. More in-depth discussions on them are available in *How Trends Make You A Smarter Investor*.

As already mentioned, the book you hold in your hands either in paperback or ebook format is about recognizing, finding, and then owning the right real estate investment for you. It explains various investment categories and focuses on developing the marketing systems to locate them.

Successful marketing underlies successful real estate investing. Yet, marketing is a broad term which we will discuss in further detail alongside various approaches to uncovering real estate investment opportunities.

And although the subject of this book is about finding profitable real estate investments, its information is transferable to regular real estate buyers and sellers.

Readers learn the steps to analyze these investments, but the information is not final or complete. If learning more about topics in this book interests you, look for an upcoming title in this series.

Real estate investing, its many opportunities, possibilities, and aspects, is a subject that spans a wide range.

*Finding Profitable Deals concludes* with several other important considerations for real estate investors and provides a resource section at the end.

This book aims to contribute to a vast body of knowledge from the perspective of a real estate veteran. Its intention lies in offering fresh perspectives about the real estate investing business. It brings together information that investors usually find piecemeal. The idea is to make investors' lives easier and more straightforward.

Let it stimulate your desire for more, then put you on the path to excelling in the investments that best align with you.

Happy Investing!

*Patience and perseverance have a magical effect before which difficulties disappear and obstacles vanish.*

*— John Quincy Adams.*

# CHAPTER 1

# MARKETS & OPPORTUNITIES

Real estate investing is a business which, like any other business, requires buyers and sellers of property. Think of the real estate professionals, whether real estate agents, real estate attorneys, or mortgage professionals, as facilitators between buyers and sellers they must somehow find. Real estate investors must identify and locate them as well, without exception.

All markets, the opportunities they offer, and the potential profits which derive from the markets and the opportunities comprise buyers and sellers. Behind any property stands the party which owns it, the potential seller. Buyers may already own property (or not). Their interest in buying real estate lies in the desire to generate profits. Any party can be both a buyer and a seller.

A party who is a buyer today may be a seller tomorrow. Therefore, anyone who wishes to invest in real estate must know how and where to find sellers and buyers for any property category. The questions then become how best to do so, where to focus, and how to pursue this goal.

This chapter details several ways to identify markets, recognize opportunities, and find leads.

Because you, the real estate investor, must decide what most resonates with you and your aims, the content implies no endorsements. Once you encounter what resonates with you, it will be easier to proceed and to assess any other missing pieces. With further information, training, and experience you may even become a master in certain investment categories.

But before listing the many sources to find great real estate properties, let's first mention specializing in a niche market. All categories are niche markets and those niche markets have sub-niches. Niche markets benefit real estate investors because they provide specialization and therefore differentiation in the wide world of real estate.

Once you decide which type of property to invest in and what that property looks like, you will be miles ahead of the competition. That could mean you focus on fixers, on properties in original condition or on turnkey properties.

When you become knowledgeable about your chosen category, meaning you understand its distinctions, idiosyncrasies, opportunities, and numbers, you will succeed. But let's move on to the next big question.

## Which Markets to Invest In?

Perhaps the number one question for real estate investors is the question which markets to invest in. The question stems from a fear of making a mistake, a human trait. After all, many real estate investments cost princely sums of money, though what is a big sum to one person might be little to another.

The question is, therefore, more about how to avoid making mistakes, how to mitigate risk, and how to succeed, all aspects that warrant much consideration. Read more about these subjects in the first book of this series. It addresses them in deeper ways. They represent fundamentals any real estate investor must master.

Where to invest in real estate can often be the biggest obstacle for real estate investors to move forward.

Which real estate markets to invest in presents a conundrum for many investors. Some investors live in high cost-of-living areas where specialized investment strategies such as flipping properties can produce excellent results. However, cash flow often is elusive or negative in such areas.

Other investors have little available cash or little knowledge of real estate markets. Plus, other unknowns exist. They include how to manage the investment, how to run a business and many others.

The good news is that real estate opportunities present themselves once you network. Some good places to start are real estate investment groups (REIs) and local real estate investment groups. Although you can join virtual REI groups like BiggerPockets, it is better to start with a local group or a chapter of the National Real Estate Investors Association.

Virtual platforms are large and sell investors on anything from membership to books, to webinars, to seminars, to real estate opportunities. While most local groups offer the same items, it is easier for investors to interact and to discern what is what. Then, consider joining virtual platforms as well. In either you will get to know fellow investors, trends, and some market data.

Also, consider becoming a member of associations that relate to your investing interests. For a multi-family investor, the local apartment owners' association can add much value. In addition, multi-family investors ought to learn about local tenancy laws, information which local rent boards provide.

Real estate investing is a field in which education pays a lot of money, but real estate investor training, seminars or conferences are entry points only. There is always more to learn and more to become. Learning inspires you, right?

If you are like most investors, starting online is the natural first step. It is easy to locate anything real estate investment related online, on Craigslist, Zillow, Trulia, LoopNet, and the list goes on. But online searches supply superficial information only.

And as you search for information, property, and opportunity, you will meet more sophisticated investors who offer you properties they found or rehabbed. These investors capitalize on others wanting investments without knowing how to find them. They also know that uncertainty creates inertia.

Do their investment offerings meet the opportunity and profit criteria? Sometimes yes. Sometimes no. Only you know what works for you, so long as you are realistic. What this means is for you to do your homework on the other party and the property.

Never take someone else's word to relieve you of your responsibility to do your own analysis. Remember, the magic words are due diligence. And because due diligence is so important, chapter 4 brings it to life.

Back to our discussion about more sophisticated real estate investors. These investors know that paralysis can strike when fear of making a mistake combined with the wish to make a tidy profit is present. This combination leads to suspending good judgment.

Therefore, always scrutinize the solutions such parties propose, whether they are expensive training opportunities, bird-dogging opportunities, mentoring deals which split the profits, and variations on these themes. Experienced investors also sell properties, notes, tax liens or deeds, and any other real estate investment to newbie investors. Reasons for this may include properties they no longer want or ones that require different strategies.

Some of these offerings are bona fide and provide excellent educational immersion to new real estate investors. Just know that shady outfits and individuals clutter the field. Relying on mentors works well when the mentor takes a true, deep interest in the protégé. Otherwise, it can become an expensive trap.

The moral here is to make true business decisions versus hoping for the best. The message bears repeating: do not leave your due diligence and decision-making to other people, no matter how sophisticated and successful they are or appear!

This may seem tangential, but it is powerful because it helps you learn all you can, then putting together a plan and sticking to it. Resist the urge to jump into real estate investing until you have done some homework.

And although conventional wisdom says you must be an action taker, this half-truth can hurt you just as much as it can propel to real estate riches. No one talks about real estate poverty - and for good reason, because we rarely listen to the unsuccessful.

Yet real estate poverty exists. Smart investors consider this possibility in order not to go there. Doing so serves them well. It aligns the personal qualities necessary with an investor's dreams of financial freedom.

Now, let's return to the original question about where to invest in real estate?

The short answer about which real estate market or markets to invest in is the market you know and the one that passes your investor checklist. Locating excellent and profitable real estate investments can be a daunting task, even more so for brand-new real estate investor. It is not clear what makes a great investment.

While there are many properties to choose from, locating an excellent real estate investment is akin to panning for gold. Doing so requires a plan, a system, and several invaluable personal traits.

I have already mentioned the value of a plan. Both help direct real estate investors' lives. Lacking either is like being at sea in a ship without a rudder. Both these success elements receive in-depth treatment in the first volume of this series.

Assuming a plan and an exit strategy are in place, finding the right investment is the first logical step. So how to do that? What qualifies?

You may have heard the phrase, "the deals are all around you" and this remains true even in high-value real estate markets like those in most urban centers. The numbers for a property are different in different markets. Remember all markets have sub-markets.

## High-Property-Value Markets

Let's start with the high-end markets like San Francisco, Seattle, and New York City. Do deals exist in such markets?

They do. Sometimes. However, conventional deal sources, such as foreclosures (REOs), short sales, bankruptcy sales, and For-Sale-By-Owner listings are few in these markets. In real estate markets where median home prices hover at or above a million dollars, most new homeowners have financial wherewithal. That means fewer short sales, foreclosures, bankruptcy and IRS sales occur in high-property-value markets.

When and if you locate them, high competition drives their prices to market prices and higher most of the time. You, therefore, must be diligent, analyze each listing, and move on the few that represent a bargain. This process takes time, patience, knowledge, work, and the ability to act.

Probate sales are the exception because they can offer wonderful bargains. Those who have owned homes in high-property value markets for a long time have a place to live, maybe a place to rent out, and access to their home's increasing home equity. Unless they use their homes as piggy banks or practice other unsound financial management, their homes will sell at market value or more. That is true even for fixer-upper properties.

While homeowners in high-property-value markets are sophisticated and know what they have, sophistication sometimes bleeds into greed. Sometimes the market corrects such attitudes.

For Sale By Owner listings (FSBO) are rare in high property value markets because homeowners stand to make healthy profits even when paying real estate commissions. And selling through a real estate agent exposes their home to the entire hot market with all the buyers for their home. This stands in stark contrast to posting their property on Craigslist and even on For-Sale-By-Owner websites.

Savvy marketing and full market exposure sell property, something will return to in chapter 3. Excellent marketing creates transactions. It makes any business, including real estate investing, viable and successful.

Yet, despite the first hunch that no great deals exist in high-property-value markets, they do.

Here it takes time and effort, and deep market knowledge to identify them. Investors who can think "out of the box" and who can add value to the property once they own it do well in such markets.

Investors who equate deals with below market prices are up for disappointment in expensive markets. It may be that experienced, sophisticated investors best qualify to enter these markets.

In the high-end San Francisco market, a rather deceptive listing price strategy continues. Some real estate agents list homes as far below as 30 to 40% of what the property is worth to drive competition.

The strategy ensures competition to drive up the selling price. Many real estate agents use this strategy, then pat themselves on the back for having sold the home above the asking price!

Amazing. No wonder consumers detest that practice. Yet, gimmicks draw attention. The practice continues to work.

Recently, an agent advertised his listing with the listing price followed by the line: "real pricing."

The idea was to attract buyers who could and would pay the advertised price for the home. This real estate agent sought to stand apart from the competition with truth in advertising.

## Lower Value Property Markets

Now let's look at property in other, lower property value markets.

When looking at different markets they will appear cheap compared to high-cost-of-living areas and high-property-value markets like San Francisco, New York City, and other major metropolises. But cheap does not equal value.

Assessing the true value of a property stands in relation to the property's real estate market, which has micro-markets. Understanding this and acting under it makes a huge difference in an investor's success.

Realize that low- or lower-priced property markets are so for a reason. Such markets often are in locations with few or no jobs, with the population decreasing versus increasing and so on. Low- or lower-priced markets have less vibrant and diversified economies.

While some low- or lower-priced markets exist in high-property-value cities and their surrounding suburbs, they are in disadvantaged neighborhoods or even in "war zones." Such locations present special challenges for investors as regards maintenance and resales.

Short sales and foreclosures may be plentiful in such markets. If these properties are in markets whose economies are poor, investors must understand the accompanying challenges and mitigate them. They must have a plan for their properties because the market in the area may fail them.

That said, some lower-value property markets will become high-property price markets. Areas under consideration and/or development for Amazon warehouses offer one such example. Vacation properties intended as short-term rentals–think Airbnb– in areas that attract large numbers of travelers are another example. College and university towns are yet another.

If a low- or lower-value property market's trajectory is one of growth, investors must investigate the growth, its projections, and its trends. Once complete, other metrics, such as jobs, infrastructure, taxes, and others must follow.

Why all this work when the trend seems obvious?

The short answer is that trends change. Big employers change their minds and pull out. Vacation trends change.

Short saless and foreclosures in disadvantaged neighborhoods, "war zones" in high-property-value cities and their surrounding suburbs offer some opportunities to investors. Cities and their suburbs may undergo considerable gentrification. Investors must analyze such properties considering those trends to ensure profitable investments.

As a side note, the more gentrification has already happened, the less opportunity and the higher the price for properties.

However, gentrification, its implications, and its consequences may offer other real estate investment opportunities. Storage units, retail properties, hotels may be investments worth consideration. And since everyone needs a place to live, multi-family buildings and the building of affordable housing present other opportunities to investors.

Now, let's go into ways to locate property bargains, many of which help eliminate competition.

## Resources for Securing Great Deals

My first book *How Trends Make You A Smarter Investor* contains a section about resources and some parts from it bear repeating here.

Finding resources and resourcefulness conjoin because anyone who blames a lack of resources for taking no action in the desired direction defeats himself. It is better to understand which resources must be in place–time, money, team, knowledge, experience, attitude, energy, mindset. Then, take the necessary steps to put them in place.

This may sound overwhelming because there is so much to consider but getting it done is a process. That means step by step. Yes, investing is a process! Anyone who desires a quick fix, or a shortcut is unlikely to enjoy investing or to succeed in it. Even those who make money right away without most of these resources in place end up having to get them, eventually.

To secure the best property and to ensure profitability, the first big step is to answer all questions about the property and to analyze the numbers. For many reasons, this alone sets great deals and mediocre and poor ones apart. Getting answers to questions about a property can be complex. And when the numbers are projections, they can be difficult to assess.

Savvy investors, therefore, work with a team of knowledgeable professionals. They do not rely on their own analysis alone, though the ideal is that they possess a good amount of knowledge themselves. A knowledgeable investor who works with others can spot great deals and make fast decisions.

Therefore, the need for identifying other great professionals with specific knowledge and to learn everything possible about the investment niche and the individual investment sets those who make great investments apart from dabblers. Find out how best to gain those resources in other sections of this book.

You may note that money has not even entered here. Money is important but the right connections and being an educated investor are even more important.

## Make Money When You Buy

The common real estate adage that says make money when you buy carries weight for investors. It means that any property the investor buys must either produce an immediate profit or the investor must have a viable and realistic plan for future profits for the property.

Banking on appreciation has little application in this scenario. This means the price needs to be right. For many investors, this is a conundrum because they compete against many other buyers. They feel pressure to make a move and therefore often buy too high which wipes out their profit and profit potential.

Profit and the potential for profits, then, is important to an investor when buying a property. This can mean various things, among them:

- Buying a run-down property in a good neighborhood, then renovating the property and selling it. The key here is that the run-down property must be available at a below-market price. The lower that price is, the more profit potential.

- Buying a run-down property, rehabbing it and renting it out. A rental property may be in gentrifying, good, mediocre, poor neighborhoods. The key remains to buy the property below market and to have a plan.

- And then there is the property that sells at market value but where rezoning and/or development is viable. Here the profit stems from knowledge: the wherewithal to rezone or develop the property versus from a below-market purchase price.

Many more examples and variations on the theme run the gambit. And sometimes, contrary to common perception, profits either come from below market value or market value properties. Further, sellers who make tidy profits sell assets which they bought at far less than what they are worth in today's marketplace. And this can apply to both market value sales and below market value sales.

Once you understand this, opportunities multiply. A thorough analysis distinguishes those properties in which the investor can make money when buying from the others. In practice, that means cultivating patience and working through many property analyses. However, investors reap rewards, among them profit, through this approach.

Making money when you buy is less about impulse investing and more about having a plan and doing the work. Fear of loss and greed also influence making money because they can inhibit investor actions or prompt reckless actions.

Investors in touch with their own motivations, who do their homework, and who understand the subtleties of the markets, are apt to make money when they buy.

## Make Money in Any Market Environment

Like all markets, real estate markets are cyclical. They move up and down. Other markets, interest rates, and global, national, state, and local economies, affect real estate markets. Up markets and down markets affect real estate investors. Investors do well to consider them and plan for them.

Although there is a whole industry of experts who claim to predict markets, I have yet to meet one who can. No one has a crystal ball, though I will concede that useful market indicators exist. Relying on those alone is something I do not recommend.

Making money in any market environment is about the right timing but note that this is different from timing the market.

Investors stand to make more money in down markets. Upon further inspection, it turns out that only those investors who have planned and have access to cash make money in either market environment, especially in down markets.

This makes sense when considering that people's lives, including those of investors, are affected by markets. Down markets may mean the loss of a job or even a home. For many people down markets mean that money is tight, which means there is no money for investing.

For example, during the financial crisis in 2007-2008 many people's homes became short sales or foreclosures. Those people had no money to bail themselves out, yet any investor with enough cash reserves could buy them and make money on them.

Cash reserves are less important in up markets because investors can recoup shortfalls with increasing property prices or increasing rents. Neither applies to down markets.

Any real estate investor who considers how to make money in any market environment and who either builds cash reserves or has access to cash, is ahead of investors betting on being right about the markets.

## Overcoming Challenges

Life is full of challenges. No one is exempt. Yet, people's ways to deal with challenges differ. For the person who feels threatened by challenges, they become bigger and more insurmountable. Anyone who blames circumstances for not getting what they want or for their life feels threatened by circumstance. For the person who accepts challenges as part of life, they become growth opportunities. Such a person engages creativity to overcome them versus giving in to them.

But why is overcoming challenges important for real estate investors?

The simple answer is that real estate investors are people. Their mindset, including the one about life's challenges, has a huge impact on the actions investors take, the results they get, and on their investments. Overcoming challenges is a deep topic and investors might contemplate the topic to understand who they are.

But since this is a book about real estate investing and not about psychology, let's conclude with motivational speaker and entrepreneur Jim Rohn's quote: "Never wish life were easier. Wish you were better."

## Identifying the Hottest Markets

It is an age-old desire to find the best and hottest markets and to overcome the fear of making a wrong decision about an investment opportunity in any market. In high-value markets, the question "where do you think the market will go" and "do you think prices will come down" and others along those lines mark conversations about real estate. For lower value markets questions like "what is this market's potential" and "which companies are thinking of moving their headquarters here" are more common.

Whether markets are neutral, cold, or hot differentiates them in prices, negotiations, competition and so on. Inventory, how long properties stay on the market, and whether sales prices edge up or down or stay the same are good market indicators. Some of this data is a look at the past and that can mean that prices could shoot up because, say, Amazon is moving to town.

The hottest markets also are different for buyers, sellers, and investors. That is because what's desirable to a seller may differ from what is desirable to a buyer or an investor. However, our concern is identifying the hottest markets for investors. Investors must be able to make money in the given market. Therefore, a hot real estate market for consumers (buyers looking for a home and sellers selling a home) most often is highly competitive. Investors pay high prices in them and profits are more difficult to realize.

Now let's lay out important metrics for identifying the hottest markets for investors. Although some of them apply to consumer real estate, these parameters take a larger view of the markets. Together these metrics give investors the power to make good investment decisions and to focus.

Fundamental investing metrics include:

1.  Economic diversification
    a.  How many industries exist in a certain market? Are they viable? Will they stay?
2.  What are the median income and demographics in the market?

    a.  This metric helps determine whether the market has upside for locals, not just investors.

    b.  Assess whether the locals can afford property in the given market. If they cannot, you will either deal with other investors, lower the price, or sit on the property.

3. Does the market remain affordable?

    a.  This one goes hand in hand with no. 2. Affordability is the catchword of our times and it is important. If people cannot afford the housing prices, they are priced out. You will sell them little.

4. Is the area attractive to new people? Are people moving in?

    a.  If so, why are they moving there? The answer to this relates to no. 1 above.

5. What is the current housing market like in that city or location?

    a.  Is there enough housing supply?

    b.  What are the rents?

    c.  What, if any, development plans does the city/location have?

6. Are other investors already there?

    a.  How long have they been there?

    b.  Are investors taking over?

7. What is the percentage of homeowners and the percentage of renters?

    a. If the market has a huge number of renters, many investors are there already. This might mean increased competition.

    b. Know the state and local rental laws because they provide an additional important layer of the market there. They also influence profitability potential.

8. How old is the housing stock in the market you are considering?

    a. This goes hand in hand with the number of available fixer properties. Knowing this metric allows you to identify opportunities.

    b. May have implications for maintenance, development, etc.

9. Is there a surge in new housing stock already underway? How many permits are on the books in that market?

    a. Understanding this metric will help you assess the competition.

    b. You will glimpse the not so distant future.

10. Is the market a vacation home market?

    a. If so, different considerations for vacancy rates, property management, seasonality, upkeep and maintenance, etc. apply.

11. What tax liabilities does the property carry?

    a. Tax rates differ from state to state. Some states have high property taxes, others low ones.

b. Municipalities, cities, and towns also assess taxes on real estate. You must know what those taxes are and how they affect the property and your returns.

Knowing the answers to the above questions and understanding them is indispensable to investors. These questions and areas to investigate are fundamental to real estate investing, though each investing niche has additional considerations.

That is why educated, knowledgeable investors conversant in their niche and in the markets have an immediate advantage. Plus, these investors increase their ability to mitigate risk.

One last point on the hottest market subject. Prestigious magazines and newspapers, and real estate agents who specialize in working with investors, and others publish lists of the hottest markets for investors. Many of these lists are outdated the moment they appear because once a market has become the hottest market, most often many investors already own in it. This drives up prices in these markets.

Any investor who wants to identify such markets may well start with such a list but should not rely on it and do the homework outlined above on various markets. Fast changes happen in real estate investing, particularly when following the herd. Investors who do their own homework may find that the hottest markets are overheated. Prices there may now be higher than they should be.

In contrast, some markets are set to become the hottest market–pending correct analysis–and present much better opportunities. These markets are emerging markets with potential to become hot markets, but investors take on more risk here. Hopefully, you see how important doing one's homework, also known as due diligence, is. You may also see that investors take higher risks here.

All this means that markets already identified as the hottest markets may or may not hold the promise attributed to them. Due diligence is, therefore, one of the many important components of investing in real estate. Temptations to cut corners can come back to bite investors. Often, they do. But not you, right?

See also: Overcoming Obstacles.

## Due Diligence

Are you on board to secure the best investment opportunity by completing thorough due diligence? I hope so. Our handy list in identifying the hottest markets makes a great case for doing so.

By now you know that investing in real estate carries risks. Some risks include market and market downturn risks, foreclosure risk, tenant risk, vacancy risk, management risk, development risk, zoning risk, construction risk, and the risks of negative cash flow, and over-leverage. Risks are best mitigated by excellent, extensive homework. Some ways to analyze these risks already have been mentioned.

However, _How Trends Make You A Smarter Investor,_ devotes a complete chapter to how important due diligence is and how it relates to finding and funding deals. A future book will expand on even more about due diligence. It is that important a topic.

The book you are reading, however, focuses on ways and methods to find profitable real estate investment opportunities. The insights it offers about due diligence only serves as a strong reminder to conduct it.

**How to Gain a Competitive Advantage**

Gaining a competitive advantage is simple, though the process can have many components. You gain a competitive advantage by others' positive perception of you. That perception better be excellent. It revolves around establishing trust. Others may view you as an expert. When that happens, people seek you out. Chasing them will not bring you the same results.

It goes without saying that you must be what you say you are and offer what you say you offer. The person who does not is a pretender, a fraud, even if that person has good intentions. Always keep that in mind and treat others well.

If you have read the first book in this series, you know that the real estate business has pretenders, scammers, and fraudsters just like any other industry. No doubt some of them rake in dollars but in my experience, their behavior and disdain for others lands them in jail or other uncomfortable places, eventually. The rewards for the genuine article supersede making a quick buck.

Become bigger than yourself and make your business as an investor about those you serve instead of about you making money. The money will be there anyway, provided the fundamentals are in place. For example, a real estate investor I have great respect for invests in affordable housing, serving a vast segment of American society who do not have the means to own luxury properties or pay exorbitant rents.

You have your own "why." Just make sure it is about something other than sheer profits or self-gratification. Keep in mind that others see you more clearly than you do yourself. If your business is about something greater than yourself, you will also be able to enroll others and attract a talented team to help you.

The team you work with gives you the opportunity to grow and develop, both as a person and a professional. But this goes both ways, so become a person who helps others win. The world of business also refers to this as developing others. But these are symbiotic relationships. No one builds anything great alone, and that includes great income.

Moving on, let's speak about your business model. You have one, right?

Once you have chosen your niche, find out who came before you there, see what they did well, then improve upon what they have done. This provides you a shortcut because there is no need to build a new way of doing things or a new system for something that is already working well and only needs a few tweaks.

Remember that successful people preceded you. You gain a competitive advantage by keeping this in mind and acknowledging those who have come before you. This is as much about character as about intelligence and vision.

Speaking about vision, once the niche, the approach, the product has been decided on and customers (sellers, buyers, renters) stand at the ready, it is essential to deliver what's promised. Nothing is more detrimental to a business or an investment than making others unhappy by shafting them.

Knowing your stuff, understanding your motivation, the ability to assess markets and the competition, plus treating others right all factor into gaining your competitive advantage.

Your customers–yes, investors have customers–remain one of the most important parts of your competitive advantage. Position yourself well to create your competitive advantage by becoming a valued resource to yourself and others.

## How to Add Value and Win Big

Adding value aligns with gaining a competitive advantage. Many ways to add value exist, so long as you see that which extends beyond yourself. Becoming a better person brings boons in life and business. The quality of understanding, focus, communications, the process, and the product itself improves in that process.

Throughout the years I have met investors who believe they add value when they buy a property from people in unfortunate circumstances at bargain basement prices. Sometimes that is true and sometimes it is not.

Those who take advantage of others add no value while those who treat others well. I mention this here because investors communicate with buyers, with sellers, with other investors, and with real estate professionals, etc. Remember this when prospecting and locating opportunities.

No one wants to deal with someone who ignores how thoughts, words, and actions affect others. Others likely want similar things investors want: more time, more freedom, more money, a better life, more opportunity and so on.

Remembering such simple truths colors your communications, even if no one explicitly mentions them in conversations.

Then something more and powerful enters. Synergy and trust. Buyers, sellers, and other investors want to do business with you. It creates loyalty based on excellence, good communications, and a quality product.

For example, let's say you own rental properties. Your goal is to attract good renters which are those who take good care of the property, who always pay rent on time, and so forth. Good tenants come to you by design. Good tenants often stay a long time when there is value. They also build your reputation and even refer others like themselves to your rentals.

For our purposes, two design components are properties in good condition and properties that are well-managed. A third might be amenities your target tenants desire and appreciate. All offered at a competitive rental price. Now you have a quality product for a fair price.

You advertise the rental. Potential tenants arrive. Guide them through a process that is pleasant and firm. Complete background checks. Call references. All these items are about excellent communications, systems, and follow up. They ensure the right fit.

When you think big and about more than making money, you become a brand. Brands have tremendous value because they stand for certain value propositions. Once your customers recognize your brand, your business becomes more predictable, more on point, and often more profitable.

But back to the value proposition, that which makes your product or service attractive to those who buy from you or sell to you. If you have read about the nine trends my previous book discusses, you may already have lots of ideas for the right value proposition for yourself because those nine trends point toward problems that need solutions. They point to needed innovations, to what people are looking for (related to real estate and real estate investing), to pain points people experience about housing. If you have not yet read that book, do so and add value as a real estate investor.

I hope you see how all these elements work together. You might glean that excellent communication plays a huge role in building a business. As do having a worthwhile product that attracts customers and adding value. It is the vehicle that makes your dreams of real estate investing a reality.

Persuasion plays a role in any conversation but pushing people to buy or sell anything has no place. It often backfires. Those who resonate with your message will arrive if you do the other things the book discusses. This is as true for finding profitable deals as for any other endeavor.

Okay, before we move on to uncovering opportunities, deals, and profits, here are the first steps we have.

See the quick recap of the strategies here:

1. Decide on markets to investigate.
2. Define your niche.
3. Build resources.
4. Make money when you buy.
5. Profit in any market environment.
6. Develop relationships.
7. Identify the hottest markets.
8. Locate property opportunities.
9. Do your homework.
10. Add to your portfolio.
11. Add value.

# CHAPTER 2

# REAL ESTATE INVESTMENT NICHES

## Single-Family Homes

Single-family homes are a popular real estate niche for investors. Most people are familiar with single-family homes and have some idea of their local single-family home market. Single-family homes require little knowledge or skill. They are easy entry points.

For this reason, they appeal to beginning investors, yet intense competition renders this niche more difficult. Thus, single-family homes often change hands at market prices. And market prices are retail prices.

Single-family homes also pose special problems. For instance, should the property sit vacant for some time, income stops. In that case, the home also becomes an easy target for vandalism.

Anyone who wants to invest in single-family homes might consider a different angle. That could mean specializing only in homes that have equity or in becoming an expert in second mortgages in a given market. In addition, it is good to know all sub-market information because sometimes a home one block away from another has a different value.

Many investors who enjoy single-family homes as investments often have several homes in the same area. In that scenario, managing the properties and generating income become easier because this approach mitigates risk.

Single-family homes can be great investments as long as investors know the market and have a plan.

**Multi-Family**

The darlings of real estate investing, multi-family homes offer the ability to have several income streams from the same asset. For instance, if you own a 3-unit building you could live in one unit and rent out the other two. If you were to rent out all three units but one of them were to remain vacant, you would still receive two rent payments. In contrast, a vacant single-family home provides no income.

House hacking, a recent term, has gained popularity in a world where making ends meet and the desire to get ahead often stand at odds. When house hacking, the investor owns a fixer in which he also lives. Let's assume it is a 3-unit fixer. He rents out the other units to rehab the property. This gives him a place to live. In the best scenario, the other two units are paying his rent and mortgage. It also gives him an income stream.

House hacking centers on the idea that the investor moves on once the renovation is complete, and either sells the building or keeps it as an income property. This may be an ideal solution for some investors, so long as they are fine with living in the same property as their renters.

Ideally, the house hacking investor stays until the remodel is complete, a year on average. The investor manages everything himself versus engaging (and paying for) a property management company.

Multi-family buildings encompass a wide variety. Small, mid-size, and large apartment buildings all fall under this umbrella term.

Multi-family buildings, including apartment buildings, are subject to landlord-tenant laws of the state, the county, and the municipality they are in. Knowing and understanding landlord-tenant law for the state and location you invest in is a MUST. Anyone who skips this step puts the investment and their financial future at risk.

The fundamental evaluation of a small multi-family building which has from 2 to 6 units and 5-12-unit apartment buildings is similar to that of single-family homes. However, the financial analysis is more involved. Rent rolls and tax returns are important components of this analysis. Buyers may refer to the property's rent roll in the seller's disclosures. In case they are not in the disclosures, ask the seller or his agent to provide them.

Apartment buildings where current owners, now sellers, have not raised rents in a long time can offer excellent upside to investors.

Some multi-family buildings have vacant units or are vacant and the seller and their representative often provide projections. Many such projections are rose-colored or faulty, so run your own numbers.

Mid-size apartment buildings range from 13 to 99 units. Large-size apartment buildings have over 100 units. The economy of scale applies both to mid-size and large-size apartment buildings. It represents savings to the investor. Larger unit-size mitigates vacancy losses in such buildings. It also equates to lower property management, tax, insurance, and maintenance costs. Overall, this means lower per unit costs and higher profits. Think cash flow.

Large- and mid-size apartment buildings often also are easier to finance. Financing for 2-6-unit buildings is like that for single-family homes, while lenders finance mid- to large-size apartment buildings by analyzing the building's income. In addition, investors can own such buildings with less equity either as an individual investor or by having other investor partners.

One would think these facts translate to owning apartment buildings with the most units possible. Not so. Corporations and institutional investors bid on the largest size apartment buildings. This creates hurdles and competition for individual large-size apartment building investors. Mid-size apartment buildings are excellent alternatives.

As already mentioned, analysis of multi-family properties with over six units relies on rent rolls, the seller's tax return, and improvement or upgrade possibilities. All other due diligence components are necessary, and market knowledge goes a long way.

Any investor can start the analysis by the usual means–via online sources, tax records, marketing materials if they exist, and so on. But investors who value their time and other resources engage knowledgeable real estate agents because commercial properties like these require a long list of items for correct analysis. Excellent commercial brokers also understand how to write contracts and can make recommendations about the best way to manage the property.

Most mid- and large-size apartment buildings require professional property management. Choosing the best property management companies is yet another important ingredient in owning apartment buildings. Details of how to choose the best property management company are beyond this book. A whole separate process for managing multi-family and apartment buildings exists. Investors do well to examine property management options before owning a building. Consult Appendix A.

## Short-Term Rentals

In contrast to most multi-family and apartment investing, short-term rental properties have captured the imagination of investors over the past few years.

Airbnb, the home sharing platform started by a former San Francisco renter, changed the rental, vacation rental, and hotel industries. Airbnb and other short-term home rental platforms offer variety, easy income, and renters who have no rights. Short-term rentals take the hassle out of renting. Everything from a room in a private home, to corporate rentals, to rentals that span months is available.

Profit margins for renting rooms, apartments, or full single-family homes are much higher than what the same landlord could get in the regular rental market. In this way, home sharing contributes to even tighter inventory in cities. Short-term rentals are one reason for housing shortages. A fine line exists between profits for enterprising investors and the high economic and social costs short-term rentals create. But as investment assets they present entrepreneurship opportunities and high profit potential.

Short-term rentals draw heated ongoing debates because they present ground for ethics and social responsibility. The euphemism for short-term rentals is the term home sharing. That term conveys the 1970s communal, "share the love" feeling. It is a misnomer. Today's term equates profits.

This context is important because short-term rentals were unregulated until recently. Some remain unregulated. Large professional and smaller landlords got into the game. Even renters became home sharers, mostly in violation of their leases.

Homeowners who never before considered renting out a room in their home now rent only via home sharing platforms. Others who previously rented in-law apartments to long-term tenants switched to higher profit short-term rentals.

Renters who were paying sky-high rents but did not want regular roommates started renting out rooms in their sometimes rent-controlled apartments. Some of them even rented out their entire apartment. And real estate investors bought up what often would have been regular housing stock to get more money for property rentals via home sharing platforms.

Because the short-term rental market is so lucrative and allows homeowners and renters who otherwise might have to move on to lower cost-of-living locations to stay in their homes, home sharing platforms became political entities. They lobbied for unregulated short-term rentals on all imaginable levels: at community meetings, city halls, and on the county, state, national, and even international stages.

Venture capital backers of the home sharing companies funded the lobbying alongside lobbies for gig economy companies. Their lobbying efforts bore some fruit, but cities began to regulate home sharing. Then several cities enacted home sharing regulations and imposed hotel taxes on such rentals. Before regulation, short-term rentals were a free-for-all. Once a modicum of regulation happened, smug industry ads all but disappeared, as did many illegal listings.

But why mention all this?

Despite more regulation, the home sharing business model stays. Some real estate investors even advertise their home sharing systems online to sell either training, seminars, or properties or both to other investors. Opportunity abounds and that is fine. Any investor who incorporates short-term rentals into his holdings still ought to understand how the industry came about and how it works.

Importantly, short-term rentals are most profitable when the investor owns a minimum of five to ten such properties. With this many rental properties and the constant renter turnover they bring, the investors either must manage them or find professional short-term rental property management companies. A whole cottage industry with support services for short-term rentals has sprung up.

Owning five or more short-term rental properties has other implications still. The management aspect alone implies a more corporate approach. While smaller investors continue to make some money with short-term rentals, they may find them labor-intensive and somewhat unpredictable.

The right location and the right amenities are essentials because short-term renters most often are travelers, whether for business or pleasure. While short-term rentals are not hotels, many of them fulfill the function of hotels. That means managing them must be impeccable. It can also mean that this rental type often has high vacancy rates.

This train of thought then leads to another issue, that of finding properties that allow short-term rentals. For example, many condo buildings do not allow short-term rentals. They want to ensure the safety of owners who live in the building, to maintain the integrity of the building, and to afford the right insurance coverage. They do not wish to become hotels.

Many would-be homeowners in high-value property markets dislike these stipulations. They feel that their lifestyle could be what they imagine it to be without having tedious long-term roommates who have rights under rental laws. They could circumvent this by owning a single-family home. Some do but many do not.

Investors attracted to short-term rentals must weigh these issues and take responsibility for their choices. As regulation for short-term rentals increases, investors do well to understand the broader consequences in this market niche. While the high return and the diminished landlord obligations appeal, considerable legal, economic, and social issues surround the business model.

For short-term rental markets that attract many tourists, cities in Florida, some cities in the Southwest and on the West Coast work. Some of those same locations work well for business travelers, too. Do your homework. Run the numbers and err on the conservative side. See the appendix for resources to guide you. And follow these tips for buying and owning short-term rental properties:

- Know local rental laws and codes.
- Invest in properties in popular locations.
- Investigate the neighborhoods.
- Develop a rental strategy.
- Plan for more intense management.
- Factor in short-term rental cycles.
- Look for short-term rental patterns.
- Provide the right services to succeed long-term.
- Conduct proper due diligence on properties.

## Hotels

Hotels are the ultimate short-term rental business. In fact, we can consider all short-term rentals "hotels," an argument that more and more cities engage to collect their fair share in taxes. Even though home sharing is giving the hotel business a run for its money, which is likely to lead to innovation, hotels remain viable businesses.

For starters, hotels continue both in markets that offer many private short-term rentals and in markets where those either are not an option or provide limited options only. Hotels, therefore, continue to offer opportunities to real estate investors. They are, however, a specialized commercial real estate niche with specific requirements.

Mastering the fundamentals makes hotel investments challenging, attractive, and lucrative. Some reasons are that hotel investments require a comprehensive understanding and experience in operations, assessment and planning for vacancies, the use of scale, and access to more capital. Investors who want to diversify their portfolio and those who have mastered the real estate investing fundamentals, stand to gain in this niche.

Although all investments carry risks, full-fledged risk analysis is imperative for hotels. An investor's risk increases when the investor holds one hotel versus many. Therefore, even if the analysis for one hotel checks out, the risk may be too great.

Like all other investments, hotels exist in specialized markets. Each market is different and has sub-categories. And we have yet to mention the actual asset (hotel), its condition, its appeal, its exact location, etc.

Due diligence is key. One missed evaluation item can mean failure or success. And because hotel markets are specialty markets, engage knowledgeable, expert guidance. Find brokers with hotel experience. Interview them and investigate their track record.

Hotels are complex investments. They are capital intensive and require operational expertise. Seasoned, well-cushioned investors might enjoy this challenging investment niche and its many markets and sub-niches. At this writing, the hotel investing market is trending toward smaller, boutique hotels versus huge hotels. The trend is market-specific, and investors must investigate whether this is true for their hotel investment.

If all this sounds intimidating, it need not be. If you are a seasoned investor or if you know the hotel business backward and forward, hotels offer the opportunity to generate big profits. All other investors to whom the mystique of hotels appeals must educate themselves and first gain experience, including operational experience. Investors also must consider how much of their capital they want to put up and how much risk they are willing to take.

Historically, either hotel stocks or REITs with hotel investments in them have been entry points for investors who want to spread their risk. For those who have no interest in gaining hotel business expertise or in holding the physical asset themselves. Hotel stocks and REITs are great ways to participate and to make money in the hotel business. Either way, investors are stockholder versus owners of real estate when investing in REITs or hotel stocks.

Some crowdfunding platforms offer hotel investments. Through them, investors can pool resources and participate in an investment that might otherwise be inaccessible to them. Hotels are large-scale, multi-million-dollar investments mostly open to accredited investors. So, if you are a non-accredited investor you might be better off to start with hotel stocks or hotel REITs. Still, hotel investments offer some excellent opportunities.

## Senior Housing & Nursing Homes

The prequel to this book delineates nine powerful demographic, social, and economic trends, among them one on senior housing. As mentioned there, the demand for senior housing and senior communities keeps growing. Demand for assisted living and nursing homes follows suit. The market needs luxury, mid-level, and affordable housing options. As I write this, many more investors opt for the well-heeled. Mid-level and affordable housing options lag behind.

Senior housing, assisted living facilities, and nursing homes are growing industries as more and more Boomers retire. It is a simple supply and demand equation. All of them are specialty real estate investment categories. They require large amounts of capital, vision, industry expertise, knowledge of today's retirees' preferences and expectations. Operational know how is a must.

It is also worth mentioning that trends alone are not a guarantee for profits. Trends must be verified by numbers, market data for specific markets, and expert analysis.

Almost everything discussed in the preceding section about hotels applies to housing and care facilities for seniors. As with hotels, senior housing assisted living facility and nursing home investments carry an exponentially higher risk when the investor owns only one such property.

All senior housing, nursing home, and assisted living facility segments are solid investments so long as investors understand that the industry contains a wide variety of products.

The industry is complex for the following reasons:

- Products are part housing, part medical care
- Varied demographics apply.
- Government subsidies may differ and be segment specific.
- Subsidies may change or go away.
- Affected by programs like Medicare and Medicaid.
- Operational know how is essential.
- Require in-depth analysis and patience.
- Require patience and the desire to make a difference.
- Service orientation.

Offerings for this real estate investment sector abound but the sector requires sophistication and expertise. Investors whose interest lies in senior housing assisted living facilities and nursing homes can own any of these properties directly (with deep enough pockets). They can also join in via crowdfunding platforms or partake via REITs or private equity funds.

The entire senior housing segment represents a multi-trillion-dollar industry in the United States alone. Proceed with caution especially as a new real estate investor.

## Mobile Home Parks

Mobile home parks are yet another specialty real estate investment. Although few new mobile home parks have been built in the past few decades, the parks that exist offer investment opportunities.

According to a recent article in Time Magazine entitled *The Home of the Future*, six out of ten Americans have less than $10,000 saved. However, some 60% of Americans are homeowners and can tap into their homes for their retirement. Many will have to sell them and either move to lower cost-of-living places or even out of the country. For some, moving to a mobile home park offers solutions.

As Time Magazine somewhat disparagingly puts it, "the sale of a home opens the possibility of trailer park life." Clearly, Time Magazine considers mobile home parks and trailer parks the same thing. While they are not the same, the reporting suggests a stigma to those parks. This old stigma deters many investors from owning mobile home parks, although they are a viable and lucrative business for real estate investors.

In fact, mobile home parks can be great investments. Demographic, economic and societal changes in the United States over the past 20+ years make mobile home parks great alternatives for many renters in the United States. Such renters range from millennials to seniors.

Given these facts, mobile home parks represent an affordable housing solution. And unlike Section 8 housing, taxpayers do not subsidize the parks.

When investing in mobile home parks, the investment lies in the underlying land and the common areas like pools, clubhouses, and streets. The mobile homes which sit on the lot belong to individual owners, to those living in them. The homes owners pay the park owner lot rent. They maintain their own homes. Many of the owners live in their mobile home and the mobile home park it sits in for a long time.

Lot rents are the basis for mobile home parks. Lot rents continue to increase. A wide variety of parks exist, some excellent, some mediocre, some in abominable condition. Such a wide condition range also exists in other housing categories, where properties may be turnkey or fixer-uppers. The mobile homes themselves represent opportunities to investors as well but our discussion centers on the parks versus mobile homes in the parks.

Locating the right mobile home park to invest in can be challenging. As already mentioned, few to no new mobile home parks exist. Inventory is older and static. Finding the right park and a bargain is challenging because large corporate entities like Warren Buffett's Clayton Homes and YES Communities are buying up mobile home parks.

That large corporations invest in mobile home parks signals that they have considerable upside. Such upside depends, as always, on locating, analyzing and consummating the right deal. Just as in other market segments, various park sizes, conditions, locations, management and maintenance styles make a big difference in approaching mobile home park sellers and in the ability to own the right park.

Other challenges include operating the parks well and knowing how to upgrade them in correct, appropriate, and efficient ways. A small park with much deferred maintenance and tenant base issues may be preferable to smaller investors versus to large corporations. Among the reasons for this are that smaller parks can offer better upside potential with less capital layout and that large investors desire to scale in their operations.

Mobile home park investors must:

- Be patient and persistent
- Locate the right park.
- Learn all you can about U.S. real estate markets.
- Understand mobile home parks grades.
- Search Google for local mobile home parks.
- Drive to the local parks and check them out.
- Have systems in place.
- Have a vision for park improvements.
- Arrange proper park operations and property management.

In addition, there are different grades of mobile home parks. Just like many commercial properties, mobile home park grades range from A to D. For example, an A-grade park means that the park is in a good location and neighborhood, that more than 90% of the people there own the mobile home they live in, that the park has paved roads, landscaping, and so on.

Condition, location, amenities, lighting, paved roads (or not), ownership rates in the park, landscaping, and several other parameters determine a park's grade. Whether a park is an institutional or non-institutional grade carries direct consequence for financing the park Return on investment also relates to a park's grade.

Yes, mobile home park financing is available. Companies which offer this financing include the Security Mortgage Group, Bellwether, and 21st Century Mortgage. Start by assessing what kinds of loans they offer and for what type of park grade. Just this step will set you apart and prepare you.

Remember that even though mobile home parks get dinged by the mainstream, they provide a valuable service to people who need a place to call home. And just as important: mobile home parks have much upside.

## Short Sales

Short sales offer investors opportunities to buy property below market value. Lenders agree to accept less money for the property than what it is worth. Many places across the United States offer short sale opportunities but they are prevalent in areas were home values decline. This means the property owner is "upside down" on his mortgage.

The homeowner is strapped for cash, his financial burden is growing, and a short sale is the attempt to get out from under it all. For some homeowners in this unfortunate situation, the options are to either find the money to satisfy debts, to short sell, or to let the bank foreclose on the property. Since the homeowner needs cash, the first option is improbable. Only options two and three remain. In most cases, short sales are preferable to foreclosures.

That said, lenders may or may not agree to a short sale—or not. Lenders prefer hard cold cash to owning real estate. If lenders foreclose on a property, that property sits on their books and creates problems. Read more on this topic in the foreclosure section. Lenders have specific formulas and calculations to "work out" short sales. Short sale approvals hinge on these.

Real estate professionals, including real estate agents and real estate investors, can help lenders reach the conclusion to approve short sales. They must, however, follow the bank's processes and timelines. They also do well to show the lender market data and an analysis of the property that support a short sale. By doing so, these professionals (you?) help both the homeowner and the lender. They also invigorate the market the property is in.

Lenders are conservative by nature. They are averse to losing money. In case a property has second or even third mortgages, all lenders must agree to the short sale. You might already glean that getting short sale approval from multiple lenders with differing guidelines and timelines makes for complex transactions. Many properties with multiple mortgages go into foreclosure versus being sold short.

Knowing this reality helps short sale real estate investors make good decisions and allocate their time in the best way. That is, unless the investor understands the intricacies of mortgages, the varying rules and laws surrounding them. It also helps to focus on a specific mortgage type. For example, some investors specialize in second mortgages. They negotiate with lenders and those negotiations can have an impact because second and third mortgage lenders stand to lose their investment if the property goes into foreclosure.

Most banks short sale. It is in their interest. Lenders know that some of their real estate loans will go into default. Investors interested in short sale acquisitions should call local, regional or national lenders and ask whether they do short sales.

If they say yes, ask for the short sale department and for the lender's short sale guideline. If they say no, you might be speaking with someone who does not know the business well, or that lender does few to no real estate loans. Ask the right questions. Find out.

When calling lenders, start with local ones. The bigger the lender, the more red tape, the more difficult it is to make inroads. Bigger lenders often work with large corporate entities instead of individual investors. Also, know that some lenders are easier to work with than others, so do your research on the lenders.

Short sales are a viable investment approach. Overall, they offer investors better prices, allow for inspections, and financing may be available. They have less competition because they take time and some of them are uncertain. For investors who do all necessary due diligence and know how to negotiate, they can be a boon.

Counting on short sales alone leaves most investors without income for long stretches of time. Yet when they do happen, profits can be excellent. Consider short saless as an ancillary investment strategy because they have many restrictions, parties, and requirements.

Keep the following in mind for short sale investing:

- How many mortgages does the property have?
- The lender's short sale process and requirements.
- Follow the lender's process and timeline
- Call lenders.Ask for their short sale package.
- Scrutinize each lender.
- Analyze the property.
- Put a process in place.
- Manage the process.
- Follow up!
- Develop excellent lender relationships
- Seek out short sale experts.
- Remember short sales take time.

## Fix and Flips

Fixing and flipping differs from wholesaling because with fix and flips the investor buys distressed properties and fixes them up, then resells them at market price. However, for both wholesaling and fixing and flipping investors must determine the After-Repair-Value (ARV). ARV shows whether there is profit in the deal and, if so, how much.

Although fixing and flipping sounds easy, many things contribute to flipping a property. Successful flips start with buying the right property, which is a property that needs repairs and updates. Nevertheless, properties with larger issues like foundation, roof, big plumbing and electrical issues carry greater risk. They also mean more work and higher expenses over a longer repair timeline.

Headaches arise with properties that need more than updates and involved repairs. In this case, time is money. Property inspections are indispensable for fix and flips. Inspections provide investors with an overview of necessary repairs. Investors can then obtain several bids from contractors to estimate costs.

Other costs arise as well. Investors must factor them into their fix and flip formula. Such costs may relate to mortgages or other lender costs, insurance, taxes, permit costs, agent commissions, and more.

Keep in mind the following as a fix and flip investor:

1. Know the market the property is in.
   a. This applies to buying and selling the property.
   b. Tells you which improvements and updates are the right ones.
   c. Enables you to price the property correctly.
   d. Facilitates correct ARV calculations.
   e. Helps identify potential buyers for the property.
   f. Helps determine whether the market is up-and-coming.
2. Inspect and conduct all due diligence.
   a. Never buy sight unseen.
   b. Allows you to create an accurate budget.
   c. Facilitates proper planning.
3. Devise a plan for the renovation.
   a. Costs.
   b. Time.
4. Determine what adds value.
   a. Bathroom and kitchen updates.
   b. Luxury touches?
   c. Fresh paint inside and out.
   d. A manicured lawn.
   e. Great lighting.
   f. Refurbished or new flooring.
   g. New technology.
5. Fix all the major issues.

6. Deliver quality.

7. Start with smaller properties.

    a. Requires less cash and less planning.

    b. Less risky than larger fix and flips.

8. Assemble a good team.

    a. Contractors.

    b. Inspectors.

    c. Lenders and a hard money lender.

    d. Real estate agents.

9. Craft your exit strategies.

    a. What options do you have if the market shifts?

    b. For example, can you hold the property and rent it out?

    c. What else could you do?

Fixing and flipping requires methodical assessment and planning. Some contractors turned investors find this out the hard way. The components listed above are part of fixing and flipping.

Demands are high and often create considerable stress. For investors who know this and who abide by a fixing and flipping formula and its subsequent plans, investing in real estate this way creates personal and financial rewards.

Various fixing and flipping courses and books help investors interested in fixing and flipping to learn all they can and to move forward. As always, scrutinize the gurus and course offering to find the right one for you. The more you know about fixing and flipping, the better for you and the less steep your learning curve.

## Foreclosures and REOs

Properties that lenders decline as short sales and properties that go straight into foreclosure become bank-owned properties, also known as REO. When banks own properties, such property inventory hampers their ability to lend. Lenders only make money when they can lend. Therefore, REOs are albatrosses around their necks. Banks must get them off the books as fast as possible.

However, today's lenders are much more sophisticated than they were even ten or fifteen years ago. REOs may or may not be the deals you would expect. In the early 2000s lenders opted for smarter ways to sell these assets. They veered away from auctioning off REOs.

Instead, they began to hire real estate agents and brokers because they figured out that these professionals often produce better results than auctions do. Selling REOs through real estate agents provides banks and servicers incredible marketing platforms and an REO now often sells at market value.

For real estate investors, the shift means that finding a property at far less than market value is more difficult now. In high property-value markets, it is rare. Still, these deals exist but finding them requires more effort now. Institutional investors often have a leg up here because they buy in bulk.

Some banks still auction their foreclosed properties off, expecting market value for the property or something close to it. Note that foreclosure auctions or even approaching the bank directly can work well for investors who purchase the entire tape at a steep discount and, as already mentioned, sight unseen. Here investors can only make intelligent guesses about what they are purchasing. This approach works well for experienced real estate investors who have deep pockets. They can withstand any duds they may get in the bulk purchase from the bank or the auction house.

In case you are not an institutional investor, scour MLS listings and approach banks, credit unions and other financial institutions to express your interest in buying properties from them. This is a process because building connections takes time.

So, start by requesting lenders' process documents and review them. Yes, this is like short sales. If you do short sale investing with a lender, they may, in fact, offer you REOs. Just never count on that and separate your short sale and REO work. Most banks have different departments for short sales and REOs.

Once you locate an REO possibility, run your numbers for the property. Not all foreclosures and REOs are screaming deals.

Lenders also have REO guidelines in place. You must know all the pieces to this category because it can be complex.

The banks, the owners of foreclosed properties (REOs), aim to sell high. Today that means market value or as close as possible to it. Gone are the days when a creative and persistent real estate investor could ferret out foreclosures and approach the banks. In fact, real estate agents list many of today's foreclosures and they show up on the MLS. Most sites that promise their subscribers foreclosure properties charge subscription fees with little to deliver.

Foreclosures and auctions also have in common that all liability shifts to the buyer. Due diligence often proves difficult, in part because banks and auction houses have limited disclosure obligations. Remember, that neither knows the property other than as an asset (now turned a liability) on their books. The address might be familiar but that's it.

Lenders used to sell foreclosures at auctions on a for-cash-only basis. Cash remains very attractive to lenders because they are less inclined to loan on a foreclosure property. Most lenders now offer some financing on foreclosures, but financing may make the foreclosure property less profitable for the investor. Find out what the options are, evaluate them and draw your own conclusions.

All this means: Buyer Beware!

Taking all these elements into consideration, foreclosures can be excellent investments. REO investing requires persistence, patience, and most of all, a plan. Please see the tips on auction buying as they apply to bank-owned properties and some probates. Indeed, these tips apply to all bidding environments for property sales.

## Probates

Our next investing opportunities are probates. Probate is a legal process that happens when a person dies without a will (intestate). Some probates, though not all, contain real estate, anything from single-family homes to apartment buildings, to commercial buildings, etc. Probate properties maybe turnkey properties, fixers, and everything in between. Probates happen everywhere. Some probates require court confirmation, some don't.

Probate properties seem intimidating to many investors, yet they can offer excellent value and opportunity. A big reason for this is that most heirs do not want the probate property. Instead, they want the cash the property contains. That is the classic definition of motivated sellers.

Why then are probate properties such a mystery to so many investors?

It is the probate process that puts the breaks on for many investors. Perhaps they know that the process comprises dealing with executors who are often attorneys, or with courts. Perhaps they look at the process itself. Education is the usual requirement for success.

So, let's start with a few important educational components to clear the path to what to focus on as an investor.

Probate can be costly and time-consuming because the probate court must approve everything. Heirs or their representatives must file documents according to strict timelines and in the correct format. Proceeds from the probate also cover the deceased owner's debts. The courts set real estate commissions, which also come from a probate sale, and courts charge fees for everything they do. These items are of little concern to probate investors, but investors should still know about them because they are valuable background information.

Probates have rules, regulations, and timelines set by state legislation. Little is negotiable in a probate and this applies to a property's price. The reason for this is that the courts follow a prescribed protocol which starts with an appraisal. The value established by the appraisal prevents courts from accepting bargain basement offers.

Instead, the mandate of the courts is to secure the highest offer for the property. For an investor to receive consideration, an offer must come in at a minimum of 90% of the appraised value. - All these components are in place because heirs want their inheritance. The rules ensure fair treatment for the heirs.

Probates in high property value markets often sell at market value and even above, although this depends on the individual property, its exact locations, and so on. All normal market metrics apply. But great probate values are available in these same markets all the same.

As already mentioned, court confirmation probates allow little or no negotiation. The courts allow buyers to inspect the property and then, based on the inspection reports, to either buy the property or not. It is to the investor's advantage to assess all these factors because the property comes as-is. Next, the investor must pay all closing costs, including title and escrow fees and transfer taxes.

Given all these hurdles, any investor's first question is whether probates are in fact good investments. The answer is: it depends.

Only excellent due diligence in all its aspects provides the investor with the final answer on a probate property. As with a short sale, auction, and REO properties, seasoned specialized professionals are worth their weight in gold to investors. Look for true fiduciaries, those bound to that standard by their licenses. These professionals put their clients' interests first versus wanting to make a sale. Investors and buyers deserve honesty.

As already mentioned, buyers can review any existing inspection reports or do their own inspections, but they purchase 'as-is.' The courts and the executor for the estate most often have already factored the work the property needs into the list price. Again, there is little room for negotiation here.

The courts allow contingencies in probate contracts. But if the contract contains a financing contingency, the buyer must secure it within 30 days of the bid opening. Thirty days are not a lot of time. This requires preparation. It is better to buy probates all-cash.

Cash is king also because when the court reviews bids it chooses the one with the highest price, few or no contingencies, and usually a cash offer. This makes sense when considering that courts attempt to consummate the transaction in the least amount of time with the least amount of risk.

The court has the right to accept or reject any or all offers. Since the probate court receives all bids on a set bid date and only on that date, any probate investor is likely to be one of several bidders. Therefore, buyers and their representatives must think offers through well in advance.

As you can see, probates are like real estate auctions. It counts to assess the competition and to prepare. I am including the section on how to write a probate bid below but did not include such a section for the auction segment because auctions houses have their own formulas. It is beyond this book to include auction formulas.

Before we move on to the section on how to write the probate bid, let's mention why probates are worth investigating as investments.

Many probates, even in high property-value markets can be excellent investments because:

- Heirs want money, not the property.
- Some probates are in excellent condition.
- Some probates are in great locations.
- Probate real estate spans all asset classes.
- Development opportunities may exist.
- May offer add-on value.
- Heirs may not want personal property still in the home.

## How to write the bid

Probate courts order an appraisal for all probate properties. The property's list price is often in line with the appraised value. The court's formula dictates that the property must sell at 90% of its market value or above that. It is the court's responsibility to the estate to get the highest and best bid.

Even probates depend on market dynamics and competitive bidding. Consult a savvy real estate professional who understands the probate process to arrive at the right bid. A real estate agent can help you analyze the property and its potential.

All bids are sealed and include a cashier's check in the amount of 10% of the bid's offer amount. On the bid date, the judge will announce the price you agree to pay for the property and ask if there are any other bids. If someone in the courtroom wants to overbid, your offer, more bidding ensues.

Another formula applies to subsequent bids. The investor must overbid by 10% of the first ten thousand and 5% of the balance of your bid. For example:

| | |
|---|---|
| Offer of initial bid | $ 1,000,000 |
| 10% of first $10,000 | $ 1,000 |
| 5% of $ 999,000 | $ 49,950 |
| Next Bid MUST be | $ 1,050,950 or above |

If there are overbids, bidding higher yet is possible. However, those bids must either adhere to the above formula or bidding increments set by the judge right in the courtroom. Should there be no other bids, the court confirms your offer.

Note: for any overbid that occurs you must provide the increase to that offer price for the deposit. That must happen immediately via a cashier check. The court will not wait for it, so come prepared.

Once the court confirms a bid, the accepted party has 30 days to close the sale. If for any reason that party does not deliver, it stands to lose the 10% deposit. Consider that risk when dealing with probate.

And in case of a financing contingency, work with your lender to ensure the financing happens. Do this before you get to court. Your lender should completely underwrite your file, not just pre-approve it. The court will not confirm contingencies.

Probates that do not require court confirmation exist. The difference between the two categories is court confirmation probates take anywhere from 60 to 90 days. Court confirmation probates require an offer first and the court then approves the offer.

Probates that do not require court confirmation only depend on the seller. Negotiation is possible. No timeline exists and the property can go into escrow right away once an agreement is in place.

Probates present opportunities when investors do the legwork. Preparation is a gem. It is important to know the market, the competition, repair cost, how you will deal with the property once you own it. You also ought to have cash reserves because probates carry risk. Cash reserves are part of risk mitigation for any asset, including for probates.

A savvy client of mine wanted to score a probate property because he had read that probates are deals. Once we assessed various homes a light bulb went on in his head.

He paid for most of the inspections reports because sellers (the courts on behalf of the heirs) have no obligation to provide them. Many reports pinpointed costly issues that went well beyond cosmetics.

He settled on one probate for which thirty disclosure packets were circulating. Although this client got the picture, he decided he wanted to present a bid on bid date. He settled on the bid amount after factoring in all the numbers and the competition. That amount was the only amount he offered. He would not bid any higher, even though I advised him that there would be other, much higher bids than ours. Even though that turned out to be the case, his willingness to navigate the probate process provided him practical feedback.

We wrote the offer, and he got the cashier's check in the amount of ten percent of the offer amount. The home sold 30% higher than his bid. He never went the probate route again after that but ended up getting a great deal on one of the few foreclosures in San Francisco in the late 2000s.

## Real Estate Auctions

Real estate auctions are popular. And that is no surprise. What is a surprise is that many properties sold at auctions sell at or above market prices!

Huh?

Here's why. Perhaps you have checked out the auction platform E-Bay, thinking you'd get a great deal. When spending time to bid for an item on E-Bay or any other auction site, you learn that all that glitters is not gold. Wishful thinking creates many a sucker!

First, you notice that there is a "buy it now" price on some listings. This will tell you the minimum the seller expects. Even auctions that do not show a "buy it now" price have set reserves. That means they have input a minimum acceptable dollar amount on the back end, invisible to the bidders.

The auction starting price has no relationship to the properties or the item's selling price. With few exceptions, the auctioned property goes to the highest bidder. The highest bidder generally is the one who has done her homework and understands the property's value.

Auction mystique is seductive, even dangerous. It encourages buyers to skimp on due diligence which often proves difficult. The buyer gets the property "as-is" with no guarantees. Auction contracts eliminate any way to renegotiate.

In addition, the buyer pays a fee of anywhere from 3 to 6% plus necessary closing costs. Auctions put all responsibility on the buyer. Many auction buyers get milked. Buyer, beware.

This means that buying any property via auction is an unknown because it could either be an asset or a liability.

What does this mean to bidders? Knowing the true value of the asset is essential.

People often ask me about auction and REOs (bank-owned properties) and getting an REO or auction deal. Before going into further details about how REOs work, it is helpful to know that deals exist and that many deals go to institutional investors. Institutional investors buy in bulk. They buy allotments of properties and do not necessarily know what the allotments contain. Those deals are inaccessible to the public.

While auctions can be great for investors, the individual real estate investor's risk is much higher at an auction. An institutional investor can absorb any losses associated with some properties. Institutional investors average out the portfolio with winners. Individual investors may not be able to do so.

Think about E-Bay and sites like it. The item's auction starting price is far from what the real price or value of it is. The seller establishes a reserve amount which is the amount the seller expects. He will not sell below it and aims for more. Increased competition leads to higher amounts. Supply and demand drive the market. The seller's reserve amount is unknown to bidders.

Auction mentality, the exhilaration of the process, produces high emotions. Good sense departs. Instead, bids rise.

Some real estate brokers have in recent years auctioned off properties. The practice earned them trouble with local Multiple Listing Services because other real estate professionals complained about the tactic. Yet, the MLS, in fact, allows a similar approach when real estate professionals list properties $200,000 or $300,000 below market value with the clear intent of driving up the price.

E-Bay provides a great platform for real estate auctions. In real estate auctions, the winning bidder is the party who knows the property's market value and will pay it. All auctions work like this.

Just because a home, condo, or apartment building starts out at $1 in an auction does not mean it sells there. Reserves are in place. Savvy real estate investors know this and do their homework. They vet the seller, understand as much as possible about the property and its market, inspect it, and analyze all numbers. The same applies to IRS property auctions.

Auctions require a more sophisticated approach to identify deals, to address the competition, and to limit and eliminate liabilities. Real estate investors gain advantages in understanding how auctions work and in cultivating relationships with regular sellers at auctions. In most cases doing so takes longevity, the stamina to keep showing up, and the ability to purchase with cash.

Also see tips for buying property in a bidding environment.

## Tax Deed and Tax Liens

All states in the United States either offer interest on property tax-default amounts or sell such defaulted properties outright. Municipalities depend on property taxes to maintain infrastructure and provide services. To bring in the money missing in their coffers, they attract investors by offering them interest on their money. Specific timelines, interest rates, bidding, and processes apply.

However, states have different approaches and systems to address tax-delinquent property and to bring in needed revenue. Tax deed states sell the property itself, while tax lien states attempt to collect the delinquent tax amount by offering investors an interest rate on the money they loan. Some states have a hybrid system in place.

The concept sounds easy but has many variables, including specific timelines and processes. Sales of either tax liens or tax deeds happen at different times in different municipalities.

Tax deed states sell properties outright. Tax lien states sell tax lien certificates with interest rates set and enforced by state law. State, county, and municipality interest rates range between 8 and 36%. Grace periods and redemption periods are also in place. During these periods property owners can redeem the property by paying the taxes and penalties. In case the owner does not redeem the property, it then goes through a tax foreclosure process.

Investors who invest in tax liens, therefore, can expect either of the following two outcomes:

1. The investor earns interest and penalties when the property redeems. This is the most common scenario for tax lien properties.

2. If the property does not redeem, the investor receives the property mortgage free. Liens junior to the tax lien are also no longer apply.

In tax deed states like California, counties offer tax-defaulted property for sale at auctions. The aim is to recuperate the delinquent tax amounts. The county wants to return the property into their regular revenue stream. Tax deeds appeal to many investors.

As with many foreclosures, counties shift all liability to buyers and require investors to bid. Think auction environment, then re-read everything about auctions. In tax lien states, many of which now conduct their sales online, investors bid the interest rate down. That could mean that the lien returns a low-interest rate, sometimes even at 0%.

The question is why. Wasn't the investor supposed to make money via the interest rate?

Well, depending on the timeline for the property, meaning whether it has been on the county's tax lien sale roster for the time required before foreclosure becomes viable, savvy investors stand to make a lot more money than the county's offered interest rate. They stand to own the property for pennies on the dollar.

Municipalities know this and encourage investors to bid down the interest rate. The caveat is that only well-versed, savvy tax lien investors know what they are looking at and bidding on. Those investors are fine with getting no interest on their money because if they get the property, they net high returns. As you already might have guessed, many tax lien properties go to institutional investors.

For smaller investors interested in making money on their money in the form of interest, tax liens can be much more difficult. They get the scraps institutional investors leave behind. And those properties may be difficult to assess. Some might even be worthless.

The trick in tax lien investing is the investor's willingness to conduct due diligence and to dig deep. Smaller investors might also consider going to municipalities where institutional investors are less prevalent.

With tax deeds, investors must have enough cash to purchase the properties outright. While that is fine, it leaves many smaller investors behind because buying tax deeds still requires a good amount of cash.

Tax deed properties sell at auctions, sometimes at auctions, the municipality runs either online or offline. Although fewer investors show up to tax deed sales than to tax lien sales, competition is fierce. There is bidding. This means that the investor must have several cashier's checks in varying amounts ready. Should the investor be the winning bidder, the amount is due then and there.

Here is where to start. Google "tax deed states" or "tax lien states" to find a comprehensive list of states. Next, figure out what counties interest you and find that county's dates and rules for its tax-defaulted property sales.

To succeed as an investor in tax liens and deeds learn all you can. Training is an absolute must. Essential steps for any investor who wants to invest in either tax deeds or tax liens include:

1. Research to decide which state and county to invest in.
2. Call or e-mail the county or municipality.
   a. Start with the assessor's office.
   b. Find out sale dates.
   c. Get the instructions for the sale.
   d. Understand the bidding process.
   e. Register for the sale.
   f. Get the list of sale properties.
3. Do your research on the properties.
4. Pay any deposits and auction fees.
5. Bid on the property.
   a. Counties or municipalities have their own strategies for increasing revenue. Understand them.
6. Or wait to bid on "over-the-counter sale" properties.
7. If you are the winning bidder, wait to either
   a. Collect your interest and penalty amounts.
   b. Or foreclose on the property.
      i. Note that foreclosing requires money.

The magic due diligence word appears yet again and in tax lien and tax deed investing it is very important. Some property in such sales may be worthless and you need to know which ones they are to avoid loss. Other risks include bankruptcy (of the delinquent property owner), which delays investors proceeds, and the risk of buying a worthless property.

Nevertheless, many investors love the allure of owning a property for a lot less than it is worth. They believe that they will be the ones to foreclose on properties, but they eventually realize that these odds are low. The reason for such low odds is that anyone who lives in a property they own will eventually pay their property tax. It just makes sense.

For tax lien investors the call here is to banish the idea and instead invest for the interest rate and penalties. If the investor should then receive such a property free and clear, that is a bonus.

As for tax deeds, doing the homework on the property, following the auction process to the letter, knowing the competition and even the auctioneer can make all the difference. This sounds easy enough but takes a good amount of work, patience, willingness to play by the rules, and financial wherewithal. Smart tax deed investors also have a plan for the property once they own it.

Tax lien and tax deed investing work best when investors educate themselves first. Many tax lien and tax deed experts educate investors. Before engaging any of their programs, research them. Some are large corporations that have huge legal staffs, while others are much more personable and accessible. Choose well to make your tax lien and tax deed education investment worthwhile. Fees range anywhere from $1000 to $3000.

In summary, tax deeds and tax liens can be highly profitable but as for all investments doing one's homework is essential. Education is a must. Both tax deeds and tax liens are more complicated than many other real estate investments, something which novice investors must think about twice.

A few years ago, one of my client's engaged me for the due diligence on one such San Francisco tax-defaulted sale. We worked together to get ready for the sale that took place on the steps at City Hall. Once we arrived there, we had just broken in on an old-timer tight-knit club.

Six people were present, including the auctioneer. The auctioneer and the other auction participants knew each other well, and one buyer bought everything as a package on the spot. He paid with a cashier's check and forewent inspections.

My client has since returned to City Hall's steps for other auctions but has yet to become the winning bidder.

## Tips for Buying Property in a Bidding Environment

*These tips apply to REOs/Foreclosures, Probates, and Auctions.*

- **Cash is king.**
- **Know your limit.**
- **Stick to your limit.**
- **Understand the fine print.**
- **Complete a market analysis.**
- **Know what you are buying.**
- **Assess the competition.**
- **Ask questions.**
- **Investigate the seller.**
- **Have a backup plan.**
- **Assess your risk.**

## Land Investing

Investing in land differs from other real estate investments because the timelines are different. Land changes hands more slowly and that means few land comparables exist. The comps that exist may be years back and have other qualities that set the parcels apart from the parcels available for sale or those that have sold in the past.

Land investing is a long-term strategy that counts on appreciation. However, a parcel may cash flow as well and many possibilities for cash flow present themselves. They range from rent for billboards, RVs, mobile homes, farms, solar panel or wind energy company use, and many other variations on the theme.

An investor's imagination plays a huge role in creating cash flow, but the investor must know everything possible about the parcel first. To assess whether land is the right investment and, if so, what to do with it, investors do well to consider:

- The location and the topography of the parcel.
- Is the land in or close to a path of development?
- The land's zoning–call zoning departments.
- Is it raw land or does the land have an infrastructure in place?
- Is the parcel accessible by road or via an easement?
- What taxes will the investor have to pay on the parcel?
  - o Call title companies and/or assessor's offices.
- Determine usage restrictions on the parcel.
- Exact dimensions of the parcel?
- The shape of the parcel?
- Does the parcel have access to utilities (water, gas, electricity, and sewers)?
- For any kind of development, test the soil (Perk test or Percolation test).
- Are there any municipal setback requirements?
- Is the parcel a wetland?

- Is it in a flood zone?

When considering land as an investment every one of these questions requires answers. Otherwise, there might be rude surprises. The answers affect a parcel's value.

Many landowners either do not know the answers to the questions above or do not have the right strategy in place for the parcel they own. Their parcel drains their resources and sits on their books. Many enterprising land investor companies have sprung up. These outfits now approach landowners and offer them a rock bottom price for taking the land off their hands.

Next, the companies turn around and sell those parcels to other land investors on the premise that land never loses its value. That premise is very different from the message to the landowner the investor companies approach.

The simple reason is that land investor companies blanket any landowner they can find with generic direct marketing pieces. In other words, the companies have done no due diligence on any of the parcels. All they know is a certain party owns a certain parcel, and that is fine with them because direct marketing campaigns are a numbers' game.

They know that some owners are happy to get rid of the land without having to engage an agent. They often ask the owner to provide a title abstract or prior owner's policy, which is something the seller either paid for or must pay for now.

As a land investor myself, many such offers have arrived in my mailbox. One recent one read: "I do not want the transaction to be a rip-off." Perhaps that was the intention, but the poorly written letter proved otherwise. The win-win pronouncement on this company's website was a win for the company and a win for the next buyers. The sellers were not part of that equation. This company's formula is to buy land at rock bottom, then mark it up and sell it to the next land investor.

To be fair, the company did not include its website on the communication. A little research yielded it. I pointed the discrepancy out to the company and received an impersonal response that included the sentence quoted above—plus a brochure from the Pope himself about the ten steps to happiness!

Such a ridiculous response, while funny, points to an unfortunate double standard. An honest response would have been the respectful way to handle the issue. If you intend to send letters to landowners, keep this in mind if you want to succeed long-term.

Summing up, land investments can be a profitable enterprise worthy of consideration because it can yield cash flow and appreciation.

## Note Investing

Note investing consists of either active and passive note investing. They are different, though both involve dealing with mortgages and trust notes.

The passive note investor's role is straightforward because here the investor becomes a lender to the active note investor. Active note investors do all the work while passive note investors contribute capital to the active note investor's business. The passive note investor then makes a certain return over a specified term or time period.

When investing in notes, the passive note investor becomes a lender. This basic definition implies a more hands-off approach. It also sounds a little less sexy than many other real estate investments. Note investing has several components that investors must learn. The business has the potential of being safer than several other real estate investment options. It also has great profit potential and creates cash flow.

Many books and educational courses exist in this investing niche and our brief discussion here aims to arouse interest. It is not a note investing end all. Further, the active note investing business is a complex and labor-intensive business with exact requirements and stipulation. For example, active note buyers must find the right notes for their business. Their business model could buy non-performing notes or performing notes, notes in the first position or secondary mortgage notes and so on. They also must have licensed servicers by law. Note buyers also face high competition.

Buying performing or non-performing notes comes from cultivating sources like short sales, foreclosures, and tax defaults. Behind all categories stand human beings. Active note investors often meet them, hear their story, and negotiate with them. Active note investors also negotiate with lending institutions. For this reason, active note investing entails the desire to help others as much as the desire to make money. For the active note investor, profits often come from the most distressed properties.

If all this makes little sense now, your first step is to read a book or take a course about note investing and learn the differences. Even if your interest lies in passive note investments, learning about all aspects of note investing helps to better understand the risks and rewards the investment choice.

Passive note investors are in the lending business, not in the note investing business. What is important to passive note investors is how their investment gets paid in case something goes wrong. The underlying property is the collateral for the loan. That means that the active investor's business model and approach affect results.

The more a passive note investor knows about the process even if he does not want to conduct an active note business himself, the more intelligent his questions. Plus, making a good decision then becomes much easier.

One additional mention about passive note investing is this: some active note investors only accept accredited investors. If you are not an accredited investor, you will have to do some additional homework and find the right active note investor, an investor with a track record.

Note investing is a great addition to a real estate investing portfolio. The advantages are manifold. Consider it and explore its options for you. Criteria for the passive note investor follow:

What types of loans does the active note investor buy and service?

- What lien positions do these loans have?
- How does the active note investor mitigate risk?
- How does the active note investor deal with foreclosures?
  - Where does the investor buy notes?
    - Find out the areas the investor specializes in.
  - What return does the active note investor offer?
    - Returns vary from 7 to 12%.
  - What is the term of the note?
- Is the return interest only or amortized?
- If it is interest only, the passive note investor receives the principal invested at the end of the term only and the interest in monthly payments.
- If it is amortized, the passive note investor receives payments for both interest and principal on a monthly basis.
- How does the active note investor treat you, his customer?
  - Do questions receive succinct answers?
  - How is the overall customer service?

## Real Estate Development

Real estate development is a high risk, high return business. It demands creativity, money, and time. The business has constant challenges and whoever engages in it must be mentally tough. Real estate development is a business for those who love a challenge, and for those who have considerable know-how in land development. This applies whether developing single-family homes, condos, apartment buildings, retail buildings, or rehabbing a large project that already exists. Developing real estate is not for the faint of heart. It is adrenaline driven. Navigating risks is part of the course.

Real estate developers must build a process and go step by step. They must stay on track and eliminate any waste. Any deviation from the process costs resources.

If all this sounds like it is about the character, vision, and abilities of the developer, it is. Staying flexible, resilient and accountable, and having a contingency plan go a long way. Even then, real estate development can spin into a life of its own. Things can go wrong. When that happens, developers must have staying power and be able to analyze what happened, so they avoid the same mistakes and improve.

If that sounds like you and you are still reading, real estate development may be worth looking into. If you are brand new at this, connect with successful developers and even apprentice with them. You could also invest money in some developments they lead, though that is passive.

The essence of successful development projects comprises a thorough market analysis—supply and demand, land, and design metrics, target market desires, affordability and amenity considerations, and the list goes on.

Successful development creates satisfied end users, clients who may also be owners in the new development. Other parties, such as municipalities who revitalize sites via such development, also benefit from its impact on the community.

The mention of real estate development might give you some ideas, but it is a specialty form of real estate investing and further discussion is beyond this book. For a real estate development schematic and other valuable land development information visit www.digmap.com.

## Parking Lots

Parking lots can be great investments. Demand for parking exists in dense urban centers, and around malls, hospitals, convention centers, and airports, among other locations. As our urban centers become denser, parking gains additional importance. This is true even in combination with public transit options. Availability of parking has a huge impact on businesses.

Parking can mean parking structures or surface lots. We focus on surface lots here because parking structures (garages) are often municipal or institutional investments. They are complex. Investors who want to own parking garages need more money than those interested in surface lots. Garages are excellent for cash flow.

Parking lots are more straightforward. The possibility for development increases their value. Parking lot investors keep an eye toward the appreciation of the lot. And although surface lots have been disappearing as cities develop, the remaining ones continue to offer promise to investors.

There is a great demand for surface lots, both big and small. Either can be hard to find. Beginning investors interested in parking lots should start with smaller lots. They are easier to locate and often easier to buy.

Parking lots may also fall into the value-add category. One part of adding value is a zoning analysis because the analysis delineates property use options. The planning and zoning departments have valuable information that contributes to zoning analyses.

However, investors may find themselves in the parking lot business at the start, a business which is simpler as compared to other commercial real estate investments. When running a parking lot business some simple improvements can make a big difference in generating income. For example, investors could replace old infrastructure with modern solar powered gates or payment machines.

Sounds as though cash is flowing in with ease, right? Well, that is true so long as the owner knows how to run a business and understands how parking lots work. Cash payments predominate for surface lots even today. Therefore, the investor must consider the pitfalls of a cash-heavy business and know how to run it well and how to generate a profit.

Further, before buying any surface lot read up on trends like ride sharing and mass transit developments. These trends affect profitability for surface parking lots when the intent is to utilize them versus developing them into, say, a residential building.

Yes, there it is again: education and knowledge make all the difference. Investors interested in parking lots may want to align themselves with those who succeed in the business so they can learn from them. See the appendix for resources.

Consider some important factors below when investigating parking investments. Some of these apply to parking garages and to surface lots, though our focus is on surface lots.

- Location
  - Is the location convenient?
  - Will people be looking for parking there?
  - How else can people get to the location?
  - Are on-street parking options available?
  - Is the lot easy to get into and easy to exit?
  - Is there any construction around the lot area or any planned?
  - If so, how will construction activity affect traffic flow and congestion?
- Is the area experiencing employment and population growth?
- Which competitors exist? What do they charge?
- Does the lot need upgrades?
  - Are there infrastructure, technology or other upgrades?
  - Know the price tags for any of these.
- What parking rules and regulations does the municipality impose?
- Does the lot have development potential?
- Could you build a mixed-use property on the lot?
- How does financing for parking lots work?

This list contains important considerations for parking lots but there are others. So, as always do your homework.

## Storage Units

The self-storage market of today is a highly developed market which means there is much competition and any investor interested in owning self-storage units must buy an existing facility at the right price. What this means is that building a new self-storage facility is unlikely to be profitable because the cost to do so is too high in areas where self-storage markets are excellent. Additionally, non-accredited investor access to self-storage units is difficult. Non-accredited investors have access to self-storage unit REITs, an option which may be an excellent start.

This investment niche is one that requires buying at low, below market prices. Self-storage units offered at market prices or above are therefore undesirable to investors. Usually this means that investors must look for poorly managed or distressed facilities. This is true even though in our current economy many people rent self-storage units.

When self-storage investors find a distressed or mismanaged facility, they must negotiate the right price, then have a plan to propel the property to profitability. In this scenario, investors must be able to cut operating costs while increasing rents and occupancy.

Sites like LoopNet.com and Selfstorage.com mostly offer market price self-storage facilities but they are great starting points for learning more about this asset class. However, for self-storage unit sellers these sites are excellent.

Metrics for buying of self-storage units:

- Where is the self-storage facility located?
- Has the facility the right number of units?
  - Look for 400 and up.
- Is the surrounding population 50,000
- Is that population within 2-3 miles?
- Is the property zoned correctly?
- Is median income higher than $50,000?
- Is there a rental upside?
  - What are the rents now?
  - What could they be?
  - Rents must be realistic, meaning renters can and will pay them.
- How many cars pass by it every day?
  - Look for 25,000 and up.

## Wholesaling

Wholesaling works best with distressed property. Wholesalers seek distressed property, locate the seller, make an offer on the property, and put it under contract with an option to assign the property to someone else. Wholesale buyers either have no money to renovate the property or no interest in doing so.

Instead, they acquire the contractual right to assign it to another buyer.

Wholesaling appeals to beginning real estate investors who have no cash. It is an easy, quick way to make money. For the same reason, intense competition governs the wholesale enterprise. It is difficult to find great deals, and many wholesale deals fall apart for different reasons.

Still, it is a viable way to make money in real estate so long as the wholesaler knows the odds, is persistent and diligent and understands the market. Some investors love it and stay with this niche only.

However, wholesaling can also be tough because it contains legal gray areas because different states have different rules and regulations for real estate. Although wholesalers need little or no money of their own for this entry into real estate, they do well to learn about real estate rules and regulations for the state in which they wholesale property.

Further, there is an ever-continuing debate about the legality of wholesaling itself. Wholesalers do not invest in real estate. Instead, they become middlemen, much like real estate agents because they facilitate the exchange of real estate assets between sellers and buyers. Some camps have called them "brokers without a license." Be aware of the debate.

Wholesalers must know their contracts. They cannot give legal or financial advice unless they possess credentials as CPAs or attorneys. Engage an attorney to comprehend the contracts for wholesalers. Another way to become savvy in wholesaling is to apprentice with an experienced, successful wholesaler or a real estate mentor who specializes in wholesaling.

When wholesaling, the investor must ensure that enough profit is in the deal for the party who buys the property from him to make a profit. Wholesale investors find deals by driving around to look for distressed property, by working with bird dogs,, or by focusing on foreclosures, short sales, and probates because distressed properties are common in these categories.

Wholesalers put a property under contract with the seller after finding them, making sure the contract is assignable. They then engage a title company and an appraiser and make sure the renovated property is worth what they think it is in its market. This is the After-Repair-Value (ARV) of the property.

Once wholesalers know these numbers, they know whether there is profit in the transaction. Wholesalers have a fixed wholesale fee in place, anywhere from $2,000 to $10,000 and their end buyer must be able to net 15% or more from the deal after the rehab is complete. Other costs, such as title fees, closing costs, and transfer taxes also apply. The usual wholesale contract assigns those fees to the end buyer.

If the property meets the profit requirements, the wholesaler must find a buyer. That party is an investor who either fixes and flips or renovates the property and keeps it as part of a rental portfolio.

But where does the wholesaler find a buyer?

Some options include running on-line and off-line ads. Since a wholesaler's most likely buyers are other investors, networking with other investors is a great way to find buyers. Whether networking or placing ads, the right message or elevator pitch goes a long way.

A short and to the point elevator pitch draws the target audience and holds its interest. For instance, they could say something like "I help estate attorneys liquidate their client's assets so that the heirs get their inheritance quickly" or "I help investors find single-family homes in need of rehabbing in [insert your market here]."

Come up with your own pitch. Just make it short and pithy and remember to focus on the benefit to your target market. Also, include a call to action to get a response. The call to action can be a question asking the person you are speaking with whether they know anyone who needs your service.

In summary, wholesaling can be very profitable for a person with stamina and know-how. Although it appears in this book, wholesaling really is a way to generate and manage cash than real estate investing.

## CHAPTER 3

# LEADS AND MARKETING

### Marketing Genius

Marketing your real estate investing business is essential, not optional. Like any other business, real estate investing depends on locating real estate investment deals and on having customers. The choice of options to establish a presence and to become a marketing whiz is dizzying.

While marketing books and professional marketers abound, all real estate investors must market themselves. Leads, opportunities, profitable investments, and connections come from excellent marketing. Although marketing is an umbrella term for many approaches, strategies, and tactics, investors need it.

This brief introduction to the vast and wondrous world of marketing is about one thing for real estate investors: to become a marketing genius in their chosen niche. The leads for specific niches come from many marketing techniques. I have summarized them for each niche.

Although I advocate that you become a marketing whiz in your niche, marketing need not take over your life. If you were interested in being a professional full-time marketer, you either already are one or are becoming one now, right? For real estate investing it suffices to understand some marketing basics and to discern what marketing options are best for you. You'll become a marketing genius on a smaller scale, one that propels your real estate investing to profitability.

Where to begin?

Connections lead to business. Connections are as fundamental as lead generation techniques. Therefore, cultivate them and become adept at using social media. Doing so is essential to your real estate investing business.

The purpose of marketing is to establish a presence, which includes establishing your brand. Both work best when you offer value to your potential customers—buyers, sellers, other investors, even other professionals on your team - and when your real estate investing business stands for something powerful. When it does, you have a brand.

While you can and should have an offline presence, having only that impairs your real estate investment business. In today's world, an online presence is imperative for almost any business. Just consider all the activity that happens on E-Bay regarding locating and selling properties.

Next, consider that social networking has a huge impact on your real estate investing business. One reason is that social media allow for immediate feedback. Social media also provide the opportunity to use such powerful things as video, audio, special downloads, and e-books.

Set yourself – your business -- up on Facebook, Twitter, start a blog, run a website, or post videos. It's also a good idea to join professional networking sites, such as LinkedIn. Once you sign up for one or several of these sites–start with free accounts–then connect with people. Then stay in front of your connections by publishing valuable content. Valuable content offers expertise, not a sales pitch. Keep that in mind.

However, consider privacy concerns for all these venues. For example, if you have a website the site must be secure and state an explicit privacy policy.

Sounds like work, right?

It is. Set it all up one step at a time to eliminate overwhelm as much as possible. Better yet, find someone on a site like Upwork to do the work, unless you enjoy doing it and do it well.

Along those lines, having one, two, three marketing channels and mastering them is better than mediocrity on all. Decide which ones you most resonate with and set them up, develop them, track them, and become the marketing genius you are on them. You may decide that Facebook is your thing, or Twitter, or LinkedIn.

Build them one at a time, then add another, and another. Most marketers have between three to seven channels. Sometimes those change after a period of tracking results and seeing which ones are working. Compile your list and devise a strategy of how to develop the channel.

The first marketing channel to consider is your own website, a professionally designed, attractive and functional site that clearly states your unique selling proposition (USP). Your website also entices potential customers to leave their names and e-mails behind, so you are building a list. And a list of buyers or sellers, for instance, allows you to market to those opted-in regularly.

One additional note on websites. When first starting out, a website is less important but down the line, as your business takes off, it is essential. It is so easy to get lose focus when building a website right away. Stay on target and follow your plan.

Yes, marketing requires a plan. It also requires something alluded to earlier: to become a great marketer you need to know your competition and their solutions. What about their solutions works, what does not. Once you know this information, build better solutions than your competitors. Doing so expands on your value proposition, your unique selling proposition.

Marketing ideas, a marketing plan that details marketing options and venues, and creativity take you ever closer to marketing pizzazz. You may well be the next great marketing genius.

Now, let's see how to generate and find the leads you need to succeed for the different niches. As we do so, you notice that overlap exists between the niches.

## Ways to Find Leads

Get creative in finding leads and in locating great real estate investment deals. You can do that by reading business and marketing books, setting yourself up on LinkedIn, Twitter, and Facebook, and by tapping into what experienced investors and experts are doing. Networking remains an excellent source of leads. You may wish to jump to the heading titled The Art of Networking to get up to speed on it right away.

One more tip: locate leads and excellent deals. Evaluate them and run the numbers for them yourself. While there appear to be many properties to choose from, locating an excellent real estate investment is akin to panning for gold. It requires a plan, a system, and several invaluable personal traits. The personal traits may not be plain, so let's take a quick look.

Personal attributes of successful real estate investors include focus, planning, patience, perseverance, and good counsel. Even with these great personal attributes, with excellent capable mentors, Murphy's Law can happen. Real estate investing is a business well suited for strategic thinkers and generalists, for people who look at the bigger picture.

## Locate Off-Market Deals

Off-market deal inventory is the dream of every real estate investor because they eliminate the competition. Many investors believe that real estate agents have such inventory in their back pocket. But few, if any, agents have them because real estate agents expose properties to the marketplace to net the highest price. That is their professional obligation to any property seller.

However, some property owners are ready to sell their properties without an agent. Many such sellers have at least thought about selling their property. And some of those sellers are motivated sellers, which are the sellers real estate investors love. Motivated sellers MUST sell their property. They have no choice.

But how to find them?

Investors may specialize in one niche we have discussed earlier and locate sellers there in various ways. See specific ways to generate leads in any niche later in this chapter.

Once the investor has a lead, does that mean the potential seller is motivated?

Maybe.

To find motivated sellers, real estate investors must assess a seller's motivation. This is less straightforward than it appears but doing so saves both parties time and headaches.

When searching for motivated sellers, listening skills go a long way. Uncover what that seller needs and deliver it if you can. Note that what a seller needs and what are seller wants may be a gulf apart.

Many landlords are tired of being landlords and may be motivated sellers. Some landlords who post rentals on Craigslist have at least considered selling their building. Yet, they may or may not be ready to sell their property.

Approach them in a respectful, non-pushy way and establish a professional relationship with them that just might bear fruit down the line. Refrain from approaching property management companies and real estate agents who place rental listings on Craigslist for their clients, though.

Locating off-market deals and finding motivated sellers go together and investors stand to gain. See the suggestions and steps to find either in the sections for the niche you are interested in and begin.

## Real Estate Investment Groups

Networking groups are important components for any real estate investor and attend at least some.

You will meet other investors who are flipping or selling other property. Sometimes a mindset trap may appear as greed motivates some members. Some investors also may have an attitude that they can do what another investor is doing. The attitude equates to not allowing the other investor to make a profit. It is a double standard, of course.

Many investors in a networking group, therefore, make transactions difficult and even unpleasant when they are dealing with their peers.

In fact, the only criterion should be whether the properties meet their investment requirements. It is immaterial whether the other person is making a profit. They are and they should.

Be aware of this dynamic when you join the group but then set it aside and enjoy the networking.

## Real Estate Agents

If you thought you'd never have to interact with real estate agents, think again. Cultivate these relationships. Excellent real estate agents know and understand their market and have connections that lead to deals. Often real estate agents do a major portion of the work for you.

You only need three excellent real estate agents to work with to mine gold. Excellent real estate agents are educators and trusted advisors. While many real estate apps and online companies are available to investors, most excellent agents are not on these apps because agents there are sheer commodities.

Relationships with real estate agents can feed your business and make you wealthy, so long as you work with those who produce results, those who know how to sell a home and to negotiate.

The general public knows little about real estate professionals and fantasizes about them driving around clients in fancy cars and making boatloads of money. The real estate industry's focus on image contributes to this perception, which lends movie star qualities to real estate agents.

Without a doubt, image makes a difference, but it is only one component of an excellent real estate agent. Therefore, just seeing a smiling picture that appeals to you and hiring the person on that qualification may get you few results.

*Million Dollar Listing*, the TV show with fast-talking hobnobbing real estate agents, appeals to consumers. It's all about glamor, glitz, and materialism—a take on the lives of the rich and famous. Don't fall for it. Instead, find those who produce results, are personable, professional, and trustworthy.

Also, working with only one agent is a bad idea. Have three agents at the ready for you. The intent here is not to pit real estate agents against one another. Just understand that there might be attrition and that one person may produce more than another for you.

Build long-term relationships with real estate agents. Many of them spend many years gaining knowledge and expertise in the field. Therefore, listen even if you disagree with them.

Many of them have exquisite market knowledge that will benefit you. This includes doing a large amount of legwork for you. Sometimes, another bonus is that they are savvy marketers.

Consumers and investors take much of such offerings for granted because they cannot distinguish one real estate agent from another at the outset. Attractive business card headshots confuse more than they help. A person's beautiful smile says nothing about their professional abilities. Therefore, when real estate professionals help you and bring you what you want, pay them and pay them well. Instead of bargaining down their commissions, pay them more.

Real estate professionals want excellent long-term, productive relationships just as much. Most real estate agents are not investors. They canvas for new clients all the time. This is time-consuming, expensive and sometimes produces few results. If you understand this and you bring them a steady stream of business, you establish a powerful mutually beneficial relationship.

One last item: some investors only want to work with real estate agents who also are investors. While that is fine, it is unnecessary unless you invest in specialty niches such as hotels and parking lots. Investors who know their stuff can get the information they need, and it does not depend on whether the agent is an investor.

On to a quick overview of some important marketing strategies that apply to many niche categories. After that, the final chapter lists specific lead generation tips.

## Calls on Ads and For-Sale-By-Owners

Investors can and should call on ads and even on FSBO listings. The strategy can produce excellent results. Let's talk about why.

Some homeowners sell their homes on their own because they want to save on real estate agent commissions. This opens them up to phone calls from many parties. They often do not understand how to distinguish a real buyer from someone who is window shopping. Many of them also do not know how much time and knowledge is necessary to sell their home.

Real estate professionals and real estate investors who know of this, contact these sellers. While sellers have no interest in talking to either of these parties, some of them will do so down the line. Many end up as listings with real estate agents. In areas like the San Francisco Bay Area, savvy sellers angle for top dollar for their properties sell through real estate professionals.

In other markets, FSBOs are more common. Just prepare to get the cold shoulder and even a rude rebuff when contacting FSBOs. Stay professional when that happens and ask whether you may stay in touch with the seller in another month, for example. Call them back then. They might be more open to speak with you or even to consider your offer.

A word about calling such listings. It is best to have a script for what to say to the owners unless you are a seasoned professional who knows the right questions to ask. Without a script, these conversations can become long and convoluted producing no result at all.

A script will keep the conversation on track and help you ask the right questions and assess next steps. Just like an ad (see the *Ad* section), your script must appeal to the seller's self-interest. It also must become a natural conversation, so practice it before making calls.

As always, follow up at regular intervals. FSBO sometimes yield great results but they are labor-intensive. For those who fear rejection, taking them on can help overcome that fear or catapult them out of ever calling anyone other than friends again.

## Make Me Moves on Zillow

Anyone familiar with Zillow, the online real estate database company, knows that Zillow allows homeowners to post their property on the market via the *Make-Me-Move* feature. A wide variety of homeowners post their property into that category.

Numerous owners employ Zillow's Zestimates to arrive at the value they list for their home. These owners do not realize that Zestimates, a proprietary Zillow home valuation tool, is off by 10, 20, or 30% in either direction. That's a lot.

Zillow developed that tool under the auspices of serving consumers. Upon closer inspection, Zestimates ensure that consumers must engage real estate agents. This makes complete sense when considering that real estate agents are Zillow's biggest and best customers.

Homeowners in sophisticated markets, often high-property value markets, know this. They also usually know the market value for their property. These owners tend to put their *Make-Me-Move* asking prices higher than market price because that is what they are dreaming of getting for their home. They do not need to move but would if someone paid their way. Homeowners who fit this definition are unmotivated.

However, for the investor who is looking for a bargain or excellent value, some *Make-Me-Moves* qualify. The trick is to find them. That means a lot of phone calls for the investor but depending on the location it could be worthwhile. Perhaps call *Make-Me-Moves* as a strategy to expand your real estate investing business rather than starting out with it.

## Create Your Own Ads Online and Offline

Creating ads is an age-old way to sell anything. Anyone can find buyers, sellers, investors, and even money by placing a well-crafted ad in the right media to reach the right people.

Who are the buyers or sellers you want to reach? Where will you find them? How will you gain their attention? And most of all, are they in the market for what you are selling or buying?

Placing an ad that says you buy homes in a cooking magazine will produce marginal results, even if all the cooks are homeowners. That's because their purpose for reading the magazine is to read about cooking. This selective focus drowns out any ad about real estate investing. The chance they'll pay attention to you is slim.

Conversely, if your ad appears in the classified real estate section of your online site or offline paper, your target audience will focus in. Place such ads in papers with a wide circulation and on sites with large audiences.

If you list a property for sale, it is more important to build your buyers list from that ad then to find the actual buyer that way. Make sure you have a process in place to capture all the people interested in the property.

What you want to know are the names, phone numbers, whether they're interested in homes like the one in the ad, which area they are interested in finding properties in, and whether they have enough cash to come in right away when you present them a property like it. You also need to know the price point they're looking for and whether they want to look at the property you are advertising and, if so, are they ready?

If you specialize in an area or neighborhood, run ads for those are areas to get qualified buyers on your list. This will also ensure that you drive competition among your buyers and that the property will move fast.

Simple works best. The ad does not need a picture, but it needs correct spacing, lettering, and size and white space around it.

These items make a big difference. Also consider putting a border around your ad so it stands out more, maybe even a highlight if you can get that approved by either the paper or the other publishing venues.

Opt for classified ads, not glossy picture ones. Glossy picture ads are what real estate agents place, often because their clients expect to see them. They are not trackable but a well thought out and well-designed classified ad can be tracked with ease. Next, target your ads by:

- Making them short and readable.
  - Show buyers or sellers how you solve their problem (unique selling proposition).
  - This message attracts buyers or sellers.
  - And this helps to distinguish you from other ad-placing investors.
  - If you offer owner financing, mention it.
  - If you buy homes all cash, mention it.
  - If you offer special financing, mention it.

Your creative juices are flowing now, right?

Also, specify what you are looking for or selling. Include:

- Neighborhood and city.
- Type of home.
- Numbers of bedrooms and baths.

- Square footage.
- Special amenities or features.

Note you will have to adapt the parameters to your specific niche.

Once you have designed your ad, search for online and off-line classified ad sites. Compile a list of them and start with up to three different ones to track results. Facebook or Google ads work well because you can target them so well. You can add more of them later once you master the process and know what wording, appearance, benefits capture leads.

You must follow up with anyone who responds, and it is often better to automate this process. An automated process, like an answering service or a survey your prospects must answer, will help you focus your time on the right prospects versus those who are just curious. See the information under the title *Automation.*

The above is not the last word on ads and instead gives basics that garner results.

**Yellow Letters**

Next, are Yellow Letters which work well because they have a personal touch. Just having a handwritten note that looks as though it comes from a person versus a company makes a huge difference. People who receive it, open it.

There are companies that will print letters that look handwritten but there are using a handwritten font. Even though those letters work, an actual handwritten note works much better and guarantees that the recipient opens it. The handwritten note must be in an envelope that is hand addressed and has a real return address versus a P.O. Box on it. To make these letters as successful as possible include no business cards, websites, faxes, emails, etc.

The note on yellow lined paper is the letter and should have your name and local phone number on it. Nothing else.

The note should read something like this:

Dear [owner's first name],

My name is [**your name here - no corporate names**].

I would like to $ buy $

[address of property]

Please call me at 000-000-000. [**do not put an 800# here**].

Thank you,

[sign your first name]

This simple letter is to the point and personal. Its only objective is to get your phone to ring. Once prospects call you, you must qualify them. Use a script to capture the pertinent information, which is whether the party or the property meet investment criteria. More about this under the sections about calls.

Mail the letters via a professional mailing provider. Otherwise you will spend a lot of time you could spend much more productively. Also, consider an answering service to answer the calls. Test the list you are sending letters to until you find a list that gives you at least 10 + percent of a response rate.

Track your results. Repeat the process over a minimum of 6 months. Longer is better. Even better, send the letter at regular intervals.

Experiment with these marketing tools - yellow letters, ads, calls, real estate professionals, and networking groups–and use them for generating leads. Build your marketing toolbox over time.

## Build A Marketing System

Marketing tools and marketing systems streamline the components of successful real estate investing. We mentioned many necessary components throughout this chapter. Now, let's take the macro view and put it all together.

Although marketing systems for real estate investors are available online, most cost money that beginning investors may not have. The good news is that several free marketing tools are available. Investors then can build their own marketing system or incorporate such tools into an existing one.

Technology is a great boon to investors and saves much time and effort when all such marketing tools work together. Technology and systems also make the business scalable. Pairing technology with conventional ways to do business is the ideal solution.

However, choices of marketing and business tools can overwhelm investors. The realization that marketing systems take time and effort to build sets in. Even experienced real estate investors improve their systems by adding or switching tools.

What then is the best way to start—and continue—building an efficient marketing system?

Let's dig a little deeper into what marketing systems do. Automation is the key to success for generating leads, callbacks, setting appointments and other business tasks. Automation saves time and other resources and streamlines running a business.

Marketing systems take care of some of the most tedious tasks investors face, tasks like lead generation, calls, qualifying prospects, and even follow up. Marketing systems save time and allow investors to focus on what makes the money which relates to creating and maintaining relationships. Even with such a system in place, investors still need to do some work.

They must set up the system, a process that can create confusion and consume much time. Although investors complete many tasks to create a thriving business, let's focus on the fundamental ones, those without which the investor has no business. All others, such as accounting and tax management, come after these.

Lead generation is the first fundamental task for investors because without it investors can neither buy nor sell properties. Every investor—and every business—must generate leads.

Some ways to generate leads are via specific webpages known as lead pages, via online and off-line ads, via networking, real estate agents and the list goes on. Investors who generate leads via ads and lead pages must have a process. A prospect who responds to an ad has taken the first step only. The investor must now qualify them.

Two ways of receiving the qualifying information are through the person they reach when calling your business line or by sending them to a webpage which collects this information. Make this straightforward and easy for prospects. The more complex, the fewer people will complete the process.

Any calls that come in from an ad you placed on-line or off-line ought to go to a dedicated business phone line, not your cell phone, etc. That way you capture calls (and prospects) 24/7 without wasting time on tire kickers. A simple 800-line that forwards to your answering service or to you, if you insist, does this well.

When a lead calls on an ad that targets short sale properties, for example, personalize the response the person receives, whether through a pre-recorded message or a live person answering the phone. The message must include the target audience's pain points and how you can help them, albeit in a brief and to the point format. After that the prospect might answer pertinent qualifying questions, questions that when answered sift the real prospects from the rest.

Anyone who calls hears the same message which means a script is in place. Execute those scripts well, whether on a pre-recorded message or when delivering them life. Scripts that sound like scripts do not produce good results. What applies to actors applies here: practice the scripts so they sound natural, personal, and even persuasive.

Investors are also wise to consider that no one wants to talk to machines. Most people prefer to talk to someone who can help them when they call, not later. If you've ever called a business only to sit in its phone tree, you know how frustrating this experience is. Many people hang up. Therefore, when automating, make sure that the prospect has a great experience to assure engagement. This leads to business.

The second important fundamental marketing system component is being able to store the prospect's information. You need a customer relationship management system, known as a CRM. The ability to store pertinent customer data is important in building and maintaining relationships with the prospects who respond to ads and lead pages. Aside from the convenience of the information at the investor's fingertips without digging around for it in one's e-mail account, for example, is invaluable.

A CRM allows regular communication with the prospects. That might be in the form of a regular newsletter, new deal alerts, and e-mails about other services. Prospects can become customers (buyers or sellers) at different times. A CRM provides the tools to leverage prospect information. It also is essential in building a buyer list, a seller list, a contractor and service provider list, a lender list, and any other list the investor wants to compile.

Many CRMs comprise databases, e-mail and calling tools, and other marketing tools. They coordinate and synergize the tools— the investor must set the CRM up to accomplish this—and save investors a lot of time. CRMs facilitate the third fundamental that investors must have a follow-up process in place.

Following up with those who respond to an ad or a lead page is essential. However, good follow-up is uncommon. As a real estate broker and investor, it astounds me how many people do not return phone calls or e-mails. Real estate is a sales business, and no one sells anything without following up. It does not matter what it is. If you master follow-up, your business will stand apart because so few people do it well.

Successful follow-up is as much about understanding human nature as it is about patience, tenacity, and persistence. When prospects raise their hand by say, answering an ad, they want something you offer. Should they then never get the pertinent information or hear from you again two things happen. Your credibility and the prospect vanish. Eventually, anyway.

Good follow-up then means making the time to call, e-mail, or text prospects. To do that well, the first thing to know is the prospect's preferred contact method, followed by creating rapport and forging a genuine relationship. This means you must focus on them and find out what ails them versus launching into a pitch for your product or solution. Your product or solution may or may not be right for them.

When you pay attention to the prospect, it also becomes easier to provide value and to establish yourself as an expert in the prospect's mind. The most succinct way to put this is: generate sales by focusing on service.

Marketing is an art and a science. There is a reason marketing and its many niches are full-time jobs for many. Real estate investors need not become consummate marketers, but they must implement the three components we discussed creating stability and success.

Automation can confuse because so many levels exist. Many companies offer full-fledged marketing systems to real estate investors that are pricey. Some want to sell investors marketing right when they start out. New investors often do not understand what the system does or how it automates things, or how to set it all up. Because of this the purchase of ready-made marketing systems can overwhelm investors and prove counterproductive.

While investors need to automate because there are many tasks to complete, starting small might be more productive and a better option.

Along those lines, investors need to know what they do well and automate the rest. In the beginning they might not know what they do well until they have done various tasks themselves. This suggests both a learning curve and balancing along a fine line because all learning takes time and costs money. For those who lack money, implement the three essential parts to a marketing system.

Many marketing tools are free, though free tools have constraints.

Here is a list of some free tools:

- Social media pages
  o Facebook Fan Pages.
  o Twitter.
  o LinkedIn.
  o Instagram... and others.
  o The profile pages are free; ads are not.
- Manage your social media through an app like Hootsuite.

- Build a website through WIX or WordPress.
  - Get a business domain & web hosting (paid).
- CRM providers include HubSpot, Freshsales, and Freshly.
- An 800# is best but does cost money. Google Voice is free.
- Answering services like PatLive and CallPorter do cost money. I include them because calls need answering. Without money, you must field calls.
- E-mail automation software like MailChimp and SurveyMonkey.
- Video marketing: Vimeo (the free version is limited).
- Deal analysis software like DealCheck and REIPro free version or free trial.
  - Or use a conventional After-Repair-Value (ARV) calculation.

For those who lack time but have money, consider one of the paid marketing systems available. To find the right marketing system for your real estate investing business look at:

1. What does your business look like?
   i. Is it small or large?
   ii. Do you have any of the 3 components in place?
   iii. If so, how are they working for your business?
   iv. Is anything missing?
   v. Can you integrate what you already have?

2. How different marketing systems address your business needs?

3. If you want to expand to other niches, how will it work with any of the systems you are considering?

    i.  How big a business do you want?

    ii.  What efficiencies does the system offer?

    iii. How will they benefit you?

1. Is the system easy to learn and use?

2. Does the system have other features you need in the future?

3. What kind of learning curve can you expect?

    i.  Is training available?

    ii.  Customer service and tech support offered?

1. How fast will the system be functional?

2. What does the system cost?

You get the idea. Start small and build your marketing system. Even veteran investors often need better, more manageable systems. Also consider this when you automate and create your marketing system: automate or delegate the tasks you dislike most first. Otherwise, you'll hate what you do.

The same goes for items you are not good at and even for some you are good at. They might be time-consuming tedious tasks that do not bring in revenue, even though they are necessary. Even if you do it all yourself in the beginning, consider automating or outsourcing such tasks as your business grows.

Real estate investing is a process and so is automating it. Having a standard business protocol in place will help develop the process and guide its automation. At a bare minimum a marketing system comprises lead capture, appointment setting, and follow up. That means having a customer relationship management system, a business phone number, and an e-mail autoresponder plus appointment setters are essentials. You can clearly expand from there.

This marketing tools and marketing system overview now brings us to lead generation options. Read on.

# CHAPTER 4

# STEPS TO NICHE LEADS

We now arrive at how to go about generating leads. This chapter gives you the steps. Let's start.

**Absentee Owners and Vacant Property Leads**

- Purchase a list.
- Ask a real estate agent.
  - First establish a relationship with the agent.
- Work with title companies.
- Call your title rep.
  - First establish a relationship.
- Remember, fellow real estate investors may own these properties.
- Find them via county tax records/public records.
- Find vacation homeowners.
- Write letters and repeat at regular intervals.

- Place a classified ad online or offline.
  - Must have a USP.
- Scour the classifieds to find FSBOs.
  - Call them.

## Divorce/Bankruptcy Leads

- Locate divorce attorneys and bankruptcy attorneys.
- Develop relationships with them.
- Buy divorce and bankruptcy leads lists.
- Compile your own bankruptcy lists.
  - Find local bankruptcy court notices online.
  - Or go to the courthouse to compile the list.
  - Read the bankruptcy notices in the paper.
  - Take notes, including contact details.

## Fix and Flip Leads

- Locate distressed property in other niches.
- Buy lists.
- Network.
- Engage a real estate agent.
  - Ask for automated MLS alerts for properties with your parameters.
- Talk to other investors.

## Foreclosure Leads

- Buy a list.
- Check for foreclosures on Zillow.
- Check bank websites.
- Check with real estate agents who specialize in foreclosures.
- Check government sites like HUD and FHA.
- Watch for foreclosures when driving a neighborhood.
- Subscribe to foreclosure lead websites.
- Compile a list of Notices of Default at the county recorder office.
- Contact auction houses.

## For Sale By Owner Leads

- Buy FSBO lead lists.
- Compile a list yourself from:
  - Craigslist.
  - Zillow.
  - Trulia.
  - For sale by owner websites.
  - Newspaper For Sale By Owner. listings.

## Hotel Investment Leads

- Compile a list of hotel REITs to analyze.

- Contact commercial brokers.

- Search for hotel crowdfunding sites online.

- Connect with hotel developers.

- Connect with hospitality management companies.

## IRS, Government, and State Auction Leads

- Scour the IRS website for tax-defaulted property sales.

- Obtain sale instructions and dates.

  o Go to the US Treasury auction page.

  o Find other government auction property sale sites.

  o Find state auctions.

- Register for the auctions.

- Purchase IRS and other auction sales leads.

## Land Investment Leads

- Buy a list.

- Scour tax records.

- Develop relationships with land brokers.

- Develop relationships with other investors.

- Call assessor's office about default parcels.

- If you own a parcel, talk to neighbors.

  o ... or to near-by builders.

- Search Craigslist.

- Search Facebook or place an ad there.

- Look for websites that cater to land investors.

**Mobile Home Park Leads**

- Google "local mobile home parks".
- Locate the owners online, via tax records, title company records, etc.
- Do a direct mail campaign.
- You can also do a search online for "mobile home park for sale."
- Realty Mogul™ lists mobile home parks.
- Find a commercial real estate company specializing in mobile home parks.
- Connect with other mobile home park investors.
- Other MHP investors can help you find parks.
- Remember that Mom and Pop mobile home park owners are easier to deal with than large corporate mobile home park owners.

**Note Investing Leads**

- Decide on active or passive note investing.

For passive note investing:

- Do an online search.
- Investigate the note investing company.

- What sets them apart?
- Do they have a niche?
  - Which one?
  - Where?
- What types of investors do they work with?
  - Accredited only?
  - Non-accredited?
- How long have they been in business?
- Read reviews about them.
- Interview them.
- What are the minimum and maximum investment amounts they consider?
- What terms do they offer?
- What returns do they offer?

For active note investors:

Note: active note investing requires much more expertise.

- Read about the subject.
- Take courses.
- Connect with other note investors.
- Develop relationships with local banks.
- Decide on your niche.
- Look at which pockets in neighborhoods and cities are re-gentrifying.
- Locate a list of homeowners to approach.

- Plan and execute a direct marketing campaign.
- Follow-up!
- Speak and negotiate with homeowners.
- Follow-up! Again.

## Parking Lot Investment Leads

- Google "parking lots for sale" and similar terms.
- Think: where are parking lots located?
  - The question goes along with: which locations need parking?
- Use Google maps to "see" the property.
  - Go see the lot if you are close.
- Find the lot's owner via tax records.
- Find commercial Realtors® who specialize in parking lots.
- Municipalities own parking lots. Establish a point of contact there.
- Read the papers and look for raw land next to new development.
  - Caveat: Do your homework first.
- Search for parking associations (by state or by country).
  - Become a member so you can network.

## Probate Leads

- Buy a probate list.
- Probates are public records.

- o Compile your own list.
- o Go online and find your local probate court.
- o Many counties provide online access
- o Call or visit the local courthouse.
- o Gather the details for probates on file.
- o Look for those that contain real estate.
- Check local obituaries.
- Connect with probate attorneys/estate planning attorneys.
- Keep in mind that probates have a timeline of up to 12 months.
- Start with probates that are toward or at the end of that timeline.
- Find the executor.
- Compose a compassionate letter to the executor and/or to the heirs.
  - o Hand-write that letter.
  - o Set yourself apart in the letter.
  - o Offer to pay for cleaning out the property.
  - o Connect them with other professionals who can help.
- Use a street address, not a P.O. Box.
- Use your name, not a business name.
- Follow up is vital.
- Learn all you can about the probate process.

## Short Sale Leads

- Find leads via real estate agents.

- Network with other investors.

- Develop relationships with banks and lenders.

- Buy a short sale list.

- Run title searches for overleveraged properties.

- Look for homes with two or more mortgages.

- Master the intricacies of short sales.

- Remember: short sales are more abundant in certain markets.

## Storage Unit Leads

- Find REITs containing storage units.

- Investigate business for sale sites.

- Look for listings on LoopNet, etc.

- Look for self-storage foreclosures.

- Self-storage units may be part of bankruptcy or probate sales.

- Contact commercial brokers.

- When driving by storage unit businesses, pay attention.

- Jot down the address.

- Find and contact the owner.

- Connect with other self-storage investors.

- Join the self-storage association.

## Tax Liens and Tax Deed Leads

- Find tax lien and tax deed states online.
  - Note: most sites showing them are in the tax lien or deed business.
- Scrutinize the companies and their offering.
- Decide on States and counties to invest in.
  - Go online.
  - Call them or write to them.
  - Walk into their office.
  - Get information about sales and sale dates.
- Understand how the bidding works.
- Assess the competition.
- Register in counties you are interested in.
- Investigate the properties you're interested in.
  - Find out how long they've been in default.
- Follow the county-specific timelines.
- Purchase a list.

## Wholesale Leads

- Find sale properties on HUD and other such sites.
- Buy foreclosure, auction lists, and others to sift them for wholesale possibilities.
- Ask a real estate agent to send you listings within your parameters.
- Locate distressed property in some of the other niches.

- Drive neighborhoods.
- Employ a bird dog.
- Put out signs.
- Attend networking events.
- Post ads on Craigslist, Facebook, Zillow.
  - Target them to either the seller or to the party who buys from you.
- Get business cards that state what you do.
  - USP in one sentence.
  - State the benefit to your target market.
  - Must have a call to action.
  - Works for sellers of distressed property and for building a buyers' list.

# IN SUMMARY

Let's bring it all together with 12 major points you read about:

- Decide on markets to investigate.
- Define your niche.
- Start building the necessary resources.
- Make money when you buy.
- Profit in any market environment.
- Develop relationships.
- Identify the hottest markets.
- Locate property opportunities.
- Do your homework.
- Add to your portfolio.
- Add value.
- Profit & Repeat.

RISK COMES FROM NOT KNOWING
WHAT YOU ARE DOING.

Warren Buffett

Congratulations! You finished the book.

The aim was to provide a real estate investing resource to you that inspires you to locate the niche or niches of greatest interest to you. These are starting points, meant to make real estate investing and the many niches in it more accessible and easier to understand. You get the nitty gritty, so you can decide where to go from here. You might decide to use this volume as a steady companion, as a reference.

A salient proposition of this book is to provide valuable information for novice and veteran real estate investors without hype or sales pitches. I also wanted to write this book so investors like you are reading information without being sold on one investment niche versus another. Many of the real estate investing books on the market are sheer sales tools instead of making real estate investing information more accessible. Naturally, I also welcome you as my future clients, whether as readers of forthcoming titles or as consulting clients.

Finally, what do you think of *Finding Profitable Deals*?

Thanks so much for purchasing this book. You could have picked any number of books to read, but you picked this one. I am grateful for that.

Hopefully, it added value to your life. If so, please feel free to share this book with your friends and family by posting to Facebook and Twitter.

If you enjoyed this book and found benefit in reading it, I'd like to hear from you and hope you consider posting a review. Your feedback and support will help improve this and other projects.

# APPENDIX A: RESOURCES

Note: The list appears in alphabetical order. It is not categorized for specific niches because some resources apply to several categories. Read the short descriptions.

Consult the list's resources to implement your real estate investing strategies and tactics. They range from finding data to analysis, system, and marketing tools. The list is selective. Many more resources are available.

*Disclaimer: Companies and services change. The author provides the list as a service but endorses NO company or service on this list. No guarantees are implied.*

---

www.agentpro247.com

Lead lists and research site. Subscription based.

www.airbna.com

Data about rents, Airbnb rates, and much else.

www.bellwetherenterprise.com

Mobile home park lender.

www.bestplaces.net

Provides comparative data for several evaluating for U.S. cities.

www.bombbomb.com

Video e-mail system to stay in touch with leads and convert them.

www.carrot.com

On-line lead generation.

www.cbre.com

Global commercial real site with in-depth research and reports.

www.census.gov

Contains a plethora of information about housing, income, business, and more.

www.city-data.com

Data aggregator with profiles for every city in the United States.

https://click2mail.com/

Lead lists and direct mailing services.

www.corelogic.com

Consumer, property, and financial data provider for the U.S.

www.constantcontact.com

E-mail marketing system.

## County housing authorities

Many exist. They vary from city to city, county to county.

www.cozy.co

Tool for landlords to screen and manage tenants.

www.craigslist.org

Tool to see rental listings, property listings etc. for local markets.

www.creuniversity.com

Information and education about mobile homes.

www.datatree.com

Excellent site for anyone serious about due diligence. Subscription based.

www.dealcheck.com

Property analysis app.

www.dealmachine.com

App to help investors contact property owners.

www.docusign.com

Allows users to sign documents electronically.

**Door to door canvassing.**

Put up signs saying you buy homes, etc.

www.dropbox.com

Organize your documents with this program.

www.ecodevdirectory.com

Economic development directory. Worldwide.

www.economy.com

Part of Moody's. Information and updates about economies and their trends.

www.fema.gov

Flood zone maps.

www.fhfa.gov

Federal Housing Finance Agency

www.freshworks.com

Freshsales site. Provides CRM.

www.google.com/earth

Google Earth is free and useful with street views, topography and more.

www.hud.gov

Section 8 housing program.

www.inman.com

Subscription site for real estate professionals worldwide.

www.investorcomps.com

Membership site to get access to comps throughout the United States.

www.irem.org

Institute for Real Estate Management. An international member organization.

www.jnlparking.com

Parking lot investing (buying, selling, education)

www.landgrid.com

Property data & mapping tools throughout the US. Subscription based.

www.landlordology.com

Site for landlords. Contains a wealth of information.

www.landpropeller.com

Real estate websites.

www.landsofamerica.com

Rural land listing aggregator in the U.S.

www.landspeedtech.com

Useful for land investors. Leads, time management, etc.

https://www.letterprinting.net/

Direct mail services, including Yellow Letter campaigns.

**Local city housing authorities.**

Find out what programs they have.

www.loopnet.com

Commercial real estate lease and sale information. Some analysis.

www.markusmilichamp.com

Commercial real estate

www.mashvisor.com

Real estate investing information site.

**Meetup groups.**

Specific to the investment you are interested in.

https://nationalreia.org/

REIA groups all over the country

www.pewsocialtrends.org

Social and demographic trends in the U.S.

www.pprnoteco.com

Performing notes and note funds opportunities for accredited investors.

www.publicrecords.netronline.com/

Public records, property data and more.

www.redcapitalgroup.com

Investment property lender with specialty niches.

www.reis.com

Part of Moody's. Commercial real estate data and analysis.

www.rent.com

Rental data by location.

www.rentometer.com

Provides rental values for specific addresses, etc.

www.selfstorage.org/

Self-Storage Association.

www.thelemoinegroup.com

Note investing (first and second mortgages)

https://tools.reikit.com/comps/

One of many free After-Repair-Value (ARV) calculators.

www.topstone.com

Note investing that develops affordable housing.

www.treasury.gov/auctions/irs/cat_Real7.htm

IRS auction site.

www.trulia.com

Site with rental listings, property listings, housing data. Owned by Zillow.

www.urbanland.uli.org

Institute with focus on urban land.

www.usa.gov/auctions-and-sales

Government auction sites.

www.usa.gov/state-surplus-sales

State auction sites.

www.va.gov/homeless/hud-vash.asp

Vash is a government program for homeless veterans.

**Your local courthouse.**

A treasure trove of information. Refer to the Marketing and Leads chapter.

www.zillow.com/homes/make_me_move

Zillow Make Me Move

www.zillow.com

Real estate marketplace. Home of the Zestimate.

www.123flip.com

Site for rehabbers and flippers.

# Other Books In This Series

*How Trends Make You A Smarter Investor*

Upcoming book subjects include:

- International real estate
- Negotiations
- Self-directed IRA real estate investment
- Market analysis
- And more.

# ABOUT THE AUTHOR

Gabrielle Dahms is a real estate investor, broker, and writer. She has published many articles and blog posts about real estate and how to invest in real estate for over 17 years. She is an avid traveler, speaks three languages, loves yoga, and lives in San Francisco.

# INDEX

Made in the USA
Columbia, SC
23 January 2021